The Southern Work

The Southern Work

Annotated

Ellen G. White

Waymark Books

Copyright © 2023 by Waymark Books

This is a proofread and newly designed edition of a public domain work.

CONTENTS

INTRODUCTION vii

Part 1

The Review and Herald Articles

Chapter 1 | Work Among the Colored People   2

Chapter 2 | An Appeal for the Southern Field   9

Chapter 3 | An Appeal for the South (2)   16

Chapter 4 | An Appeal for the South (3)   23

Chapter 5 | An Example in History   28

Chapter 6 | The Bible and the Colored People   34

Chapter 7 | Spirit and Life for the Colored People   40

Chapter 8 | "Am I My Brother's Keeper?"   44

Chapter 9 | Lift Up Your Eyes and Look on the Field   49

CONTENTS

Chapter 10 ▌ Volunteers Wanted for the Southern Field 55

Chapter 11 ▌ Our Duty to the Colored People 59

Part 2

Counsels Regarding the Work in the South

Chapter 1 ▌ Words of Precaution Regarding Sunday Labor 72

Chapter 2 ▌ Proper Methods of Work in the Southern Field 79

Chapter 3 ▌ Letter to A. O. Tait about the Southern Field 87

Part 3

Special Counsels and Cautions in 1899

Chapter 1 ▌ Colonization Not Advisable 92

Chapter 2 ▌ The Field Becoming Difficult 97

Chapter 3 ▌ Further Counsel Regarding a Colony in the South 100

Chapter 4 ▌ A Neglected Work 104

Chapter 5 ▌ Principles Regarding Restitution 107

ABOUT ELLEN G. WHITE 109

INTRODUCTION

Our Duty to the Colored People

There has been much perplexity as to how our laborers in the South shall deal with the "color line." It has been a question to some how far to concede to the prevailing prejudice against the colored people. The Lord has given us light concerning all such matters. There are principles laid down in His Word that should guide us in dealing with these perplexing questions. The Lord Jesus came to our world to save men and women of all nationalities. He died just as much for the colored people as for the white race. Jesus came to shed light over the whole world. At the beginning of His ministry He declared His mission: "The Spirit of the Lord is upon me, because he hath anointed me to preach the gospel to the poor; he hath sent me to heal the brokenhearted, to preach deliverance to the captives, and recovering of sight to the blind, to set at liberty them that are bruised, to preach the acceptable year of the Lord."

The Redeemer of the world was of humble parentage. He, the Majesty of heaven, the King of glory, humbled Himself to accept humanity, and then He chose a life of poverty and toil. "For your sakes he became poor, that ye through his poverty might be rich." When one came saying, "I will follow thee whithersoever thou goest," Jesus answered him, "The foxes have holes, and the birds of the air have nests; but the Son of man hath not where to lay his head." He, the Majesty of heaven, depended upon the generosity of His followers.

Jesus did not seek the admiration or applause of the world. He commanded no army, He ruled no earthly kingdom. He passed by the wealthy and honored of the world. He did not associate with the leaders

INTRODUCTION

of the nation. He dwelt among the lowly of the earth. To all appearances he was merely a humble man, with few friends. Thus He sought to correct the world's false standard of judging the value of men. He showed that they are not to be estimated by their outward appearance. Their moral worth is not determined by their worldly possessions, their real estate or bank stock. It is the humble, contrite heart that God values. With Him there is no respect of persons. The attributes that He prizes most are purity and love, and these are possessed only by the Christian.

Jesus did not choose His disciples from the learned lawyers, the rulers, the scribes, and Pharisees. He passed them by because they felt whole, as many feel in this age, and prided themselves on their learning and position. They were fixed in their traditions and superstitions, teaching for doctrines the commandments of men. He who could read all hearts chose poor fishermen who were willing to be taught. He gave them no promise of large salary or worldly honor, but told them they should be partakers with Him in His sufferings. Jesus while in this world ate with publicans and sinners, and mingled with the common people, not to become low and earthly with them, but in order by precept and example to present to them right principles, to lift them up from their low habits and manners. In all this He set us an example, that we should follow in His steps.

Those who have a religious experience that opens their hearts to Jesus, will not cherish pride, but will feel that they are under obligation to God to be missionaries as was Jesus. They will seek to save that which was lost. They will not, in Pharisaical pride and haughtiness, withdraw themselves from any class of humanity, but will feel with the apostle Paul, "I am debtor both to the Greek, and to the barbarians; both to the wise, and to the unwise."

After my severe illness one year ago, many things which the Lord had presented to me seemed lost to my mind, but they have since been repeated. I know that which I now speak will bring me into conflict. This I do not covet, for the conflict has seemed to be continuous of late years;

INTRODUCTION

but I do not mean to live a coward or die a coward, leaving my work undone. I must follow in my Master's footsteps. It has become fashionable to look down upon the poor, and upon the colored race in particular. But Jesus, the Master, was poor, and He sympathizes with the poor, the discarded, the oppressed, and declares that every insult shown to them is as if shown to Himself. I am more and more surprised as I see those who claim to be children of God possessing so little of the sympathy, tenderness, and love which actuated Christ. Would that every church, North and South, were imbued with the spirit of our Lord's teaching.

While at St. Louis a year ago, as I knelt in prayer, these words were presented to me as if written with a pen of fire: "All ye are brethren." The Spirit of God rested upon me in a wonderful manner, and matters were opened to me in regard to the church at St. Louis and in other places. The spirit and words of some in regard to members of the church were an offense to God. They were closing the door of their hearts to Jesus. Among those in St. Louis who believe the truth there are colored people who are true and faithful, precious in the sight of the God of heaven, and they should have just as much respect as any of God's children. Those who have spoken harshly to them or have despised them have despised the purchase of the blood of Christ, and they need the transforming grace of Christ in their own hearts, that they may have the pitying tenderness of Jesus toward those who love God with all the fervor of which they themselves are capable. The color of the skin does not determine character in the heavenly courts.

"If ye call on the Father, who without respect of persons judgeth according to every man's work, pass the time of your sojourning here in fear: forasmuch as ye know that ye were not redeemed with corruptible things, as silver and gold, from your vain conversation received by tradition from your fathers; but with the precious blood of Christ, as of a lamb without blemish and without spot.... Seeing ye have purified your souls in obeying the truth through the Spirit unto unfeigned love of the brethren, see that ye love one another with a pure heart fervently." "Ye have put off the old man with his deeds; and have put on the new man,

INTRODUCTION

which is renewed in knowledge after the image of him that created him: wherefore there is neither Greek nor Jew, circumcision nor uncircumcision, Barbarian, Scythian, bond nor free: but Christ is all, and in all. Put on therefore, as the elect of God, holy and beloved, bowels of mercies, kindness, humbleness of mind, meekness, longsuffering."

"Who," says Paul, "maketh thee to differ?" The God of the white man is the God of the black man, and the Lord declares that His love for the least of His children exceeds that of a mother for her beloved child. Look at that mother: the sick child, the one afflicted, the one born a cripple, or with some other physical infirmity—how the mother labors to give him every advantage! The best food, the softest pillow, and the tenderest nursing are for him. The love bestowed upon him is strong and deep—a love such as is not given to beauty, talent, or any other natural gift. As soon as a mother sees reason for others to regard her child with aversion or contempt, does she not increase her tenderness as if to shield him from the world's rude touch? "Can a mother forget her sucking child . . .? yea, they may forget, yet I will not forget thee." O what impartial love the Lord Jesus gives to those who love Him! The Lord's eye is upon all His creatures; He loves them all, and makes no difference between white and black, except that He has a special, tender pity for those who are called to bear a greater burden than others. Those who love God and believe on Christ as their Redeemer, while they must meet the trials and the difficulties that lie in their path, should yet with a cheerful spirit accept their life as it is, considering that God above regards these things, and for all that the world neglects to bestow, He will Himself make up to them in the best of favors.

The parable of Dives, the rich man, and Lazarus, the poor beggar who feared God, is presented before the world as a lesson to all, both rich and poor, as long as time shall last. Dives is represented as lifting up his eyes in hell, being in torments, and seeing Abraham afar off, and Lazarus in his bosom,—"he cried and said, Father Abraham, have mercy on me, and send Lazarus, that he may dip the tip of his finger in water, and cool my tongue; for I am tormented in this flame. But

Abraham said, Son, remember that thou in thy lifetime receivedst thy good things, and likewise Lazarus evil things; but now he is comforted, and thou art tormented."

When the sinner is converted he receives the Holy Spirit, that makes him a child of God, and fits him for the society of the redeemed and the angelic host. He is made a joint heir with Christ. Whoever of the human family give themselves to Christ, whoever hear the truth and obey it, become children of one family. The ignorant and the wise, the rich and the poor, the heathen and the slave, white or black—Jesus paid the purchase money for their souls. If they believe on Him, His cleansing blood is applied to them. The black man's name is written in the book of life beside the white man's. All are one in Christ. Birth, station, nationality, or color cannot elevate or degrade men. The character makes the man. If a red man, a Chinaman, or an African gives his heart to God, in obedience and faith, Jesus loves him none the less for his color. He calls him his well-beloved brother. The day is coming when the kings and the lordly men of the earth would be glad to exchange places with the humblest African who has laid hold on the hope of the gospel. To all who are overcomers through the blood of the Lamb, the invitation will be given, "Come, ye blessed of my Father, inherit the kingdom prepared for you from the foundation of the world." Arranged on the right and left of the throne of God are the long columns of the heavenly host, who touch the golden harps, and the songs of welcome and of praise to God and the Lamb ring through the heavenly courts. "He that hath an ear, let him hear what the Spirit saith unto the churches; To him that overcometh will I give to eat of the tree of life, which is in the midst of the paradise of God."

Among what are called the higher classes, there is a demand for a form of Christianity suited to their fine tastes; but this class will not grow up to the full stature of men and women in Christ until they know God and Jesus Christ whom He has sent. The heavenly intelligences rejoice to do the will of God in preaching the gospel to the poor. In the announcement which the Savior made in the synagogue at Nazareth,

INTRODUCTION

He put a stern rebuke upon those who attach so much importance to color or caste, and refuse to be satisfied with such a type of Christianity as Christ accepts. The same price was paid for the salvation of the colored man as for that of the white man, and the slights put upon the colored people by many who claim to be redeemed by the blood of the Lamb, and who therefore acknowledge themselves debtors to Christ, misrepresent Jesus, and reveal that selfishness, tradition, and prejudice pollute the soul. They are not sanctified through the truth. Those who slight a brother because of his color are slighting Christ.

I call upon every church in our land to look well to your own souls. "Examine yourselves, whether ye be in the faith; prove your own selves. Know ye not your own selves, how that Jesus Christ is in you, except ye be reprobates?" God makes no distinction between the North and the South. Whatever may be your prejudices, your wonderful prudence, do not lose sight of this fact, that unless you put on Christ, and His Spirit dwells in you, you are slaves of sin and of Satan. Many who claim to be children of God are children of the wicked one, and have all his passions, his prejudices, his evil spirit, his unlovely traits of character. But the soul that is indeed transformed will not despise any one whom Christ has purchased with His own blood.

Men may have both hereditary and cultivated prejudices, but when the love of Jesus fills the heart, and they become one with Christ, they will have the same spirit that He had. If a colored brother sits by their side, they will not be offended or despise him. They are journeying to the same heaven, and will be seated at the same table to eat bread in the kingdom of God. If Jesus is abiding in our hearts we cannot despise the colored man who has the same Savior abiding in his heart. When these unchristian prejudices are broken down, more earnest effort will be put forth to do missionary work among the colored race.

When the Hebrew people were suffering cruel oppression under the hand of their taskmasters, the Lord looked upon them, and He called Israel His son. He bade Moses go to Pharaoh with the message, "Israel is my son, even my firstborn. And I say unto thee, Let my son go, that he may serve me." The Lord did not wait until His people went forth and stood in triumph on the shores of the Red Sea before He called Israel His son, but while they were under oppression, degraded, downtrodden, suffering all that the power and the invention of the Egyptians could impose to make their lives bitter and to destroy them, then God undertakes their cause and declares to Pharaoh, "Israel is my son, even my firstborn."

What thoughts and feelings did the message arouse in Pharaoh? "This people, my slaves, those whom the lowest of my people despise, the God of such a people I care not for, neither will I let Israel go." But the word of the Lord will not return unto Him void; it will accomplish the thing whereunto it is sent. The Lord speaks in no uncertain manner. He says, "Let my son go, that he may serve me: and if thou refuse to let him go, behold, I will slay thy son, even thy firstborn."

God cares no less for the souls of the African race that might be won to serve Him than He cared for Israel. He requires far more of His people than they have given Him in missionary work among the people of the South of all classes, and especially among the colored race. Are we not under even greater obligation to labor for the colored people than for those who have been more highly favored? Who is it that held these people in servitude? Who kept them in ignorance, and pursued a course to debase and brutalize them, forcing them to disregard the law of marriage, breaking up the family relation, tearing wife from husband, and husband from wife? If the race is degraded, if they are repulsive in habits and manners, who made them so? Is there not much due to them from the white people? After so great a wrong has been done them, should not an earnest effort be made to lift them up? The truth must be carried to them. They have souls to save as well as we.

At the General Conference of 1889, resolutions were presented in regard to the color line. Such action is not called for. Let not men take the place of God, but stand aside in awe, and let God work upon human hearts, both white and black, in His own way. He will adjust all these perplexing questions. We need not prescribe a definite plan of

INTRODUCTION

working. Leave an opportunity for God to do something. We should be careful not to strengthen prejudices that ought to have died just as soon as Christ redeemed the soul from the bondage of sin.

Sin rests upon us as a church because we have not made greater effort for the salvation of souls among the colored people. It will always be a difficult matter to deal with the prejudices of the white people in the South and do missionary work for the colored race. But the way this matter has been treated by some is an offense to God. We need not expect that all will be accomplished in the South that God would do until in our missionary efforts we place this question on the ground of principle, and let those who accept the truth be educated to be Bible Christians, working according to Christ's order. You have no license from God to exclude the colored people from your places of worship. Treat them as Christ's property, which they are, just as much as yourselves. They should hold membership in the church with the white brethren. Every effort should be made to wipe out the terrible wrong which has been done them. At the same time we must not carry things to extremes and run into fanaticism on this question. Some would think it right to throw down every partition wall and intermarry with the colored people, but this is not the right thing to teach or to practice.

Let us do what we can to send to this class laborers who will work in Christ's name, who will not fail nor be discouraged. We should educate colored men to be missionaries among their own people. We should recognize talent where it exists among the people, and those who have ability should be placed where they may receive an education.

There are able colored ministers who have embraced the truth. Some of these feel unwilling to devote themselves to work for their own race; they wish to preach to the white people. These men are making a great mistake. They should seek most earnestly to save their own race, and they will not by any means be excluded from the gatherings of the white people.

White men and white women should be qualifying themselves to work among the colored people. There is a large work to be done in educating this ignorant and downtrodden class. We must do more unselfish missionary work than we have done in the Southern States, not picking out merely the most favorable fields. God has children among the colored people all over the land. They need to be enlightened. There are unpromising ones, it is true, but you will find similar degradation among the white people; but even among the lower classes there are souls who will embrace the truth. Some will not be steadfast. Feelings and habits that have been confirmed by lifelong practices will be hard to correct; it will not be easy to implant ideas of purity and holiness, refinement and elevation. But God regards the capacity of every man, He marks the surroundings, and sees how these have formed the character, and He pities these souls.

Is it not time for us to live so fully in the light of God's countenance that we who receive so many favors and blessings from Him may know how to treat those less favored, not working from the world's standpoint, but from the Bible standpoint? Is it not right in this line that Christian effort is most needed? Is it not here that our influence should be brought to bear against the customs and practices of the world? Should it not be the work of the white people to elevate the standard of character among the colored race, to teach them how Christians should live, by exemplifying the Spirit of Christ, showing that we are one brotherhood?

Those who have been favored with opportunities of education and culture, who have had every advantage of religious influence, will be expected of God to possess pure and holy characters in accordance with the gifts bestowed. But have they rightly improved their advantages? We know they have not. Let these privileged ones make the most of their blessings, and realize that they are thus placed under greater obligation to labor for the good of others.

God will accept many more workers from the humble walks of life if they will fully consecrate themselves to His service. Men and women should be coming up to carry the truth into all the highways and byways of life. Not all can go through a long course of education, but if they are consecrated to God and learn of Him, many can without this do much to bless others. Thousands would be accepted if they would give themselves to God. Not all who labor in this line should depend upon the conferences for support. Let those who can do so give their time and what ability they have, let them be messengers of God's grace, their hearts throbbing in unison with Christ's great heart of love, their ears open to hear the Macedonian cry.

The whole church needs to be imbued with the missionary spirit, then there will be many to work unselfishly in various ways as they can, without being salaried. There is altogether too much dependence on machinery, on mechanical working. Machinery is good in its place, but do not allow it to become too complicated. I tell you that in many cases it has retarded the work, and kept out laborers who in their line could have accomplished far more than has been done by the minister who depends on sermonizing more than on ministry. Young men need to catch the missionary spirit, to be thoroughly imbued with the spirit of the message,

"Put ye on the Lord Jesus Christ, and make no provision for the flesh to fulfil the lusts thereof." Work in any capacity, work where God leads you, in the line best suited to your talents and best adapted to reach classes that have hitherto been sadly neglected. This kind of labor will develop intellectual and moral power and adaptability to the work.

You must have the grace and love of God in order to succeed. The strength and spirituality of the people of God are manifest by the distinctness of the line of demarcation which separates them from the world. The people of the world are characterized by love for earthly things; they act selfishly, regardless of the principles which Christ has set forth in His life. Christians will manifest the self-sacrificing spirit of Christ in their work, in connection with every branch of the cause. They will do this heartily, not by halves. They will not study their own aggrandizement nor manifest respect of persons. They will not, cannot, live in luxury and self-indulgence while there are suffering ones around them. They cannot by their practice sanction any phase of oppression or injustice to the least child of humanity. There are to be like Christ, to relinquish all selfish delights, all unholy passions, all that love of applause which is the food of the world. They will be willing to be humble and unknown, and to sacrifice even life itself for Christ's sake. By a well-ordered life and godly conversation they will condemn the folly, the impenitence, the idolatry, the iniquitous practices of the world.

The converting power of God must work a transformation of character in many who claim to believe the present truth, or they cannot fulfill the purpose of God. They are hearers but not doers of the word. Pure, unworldly benevolence will be developed in all who make Christ their personal Savior. There needs to be far less of self and more of Jesus. The church of Christ is ordained of God that its members shall be representatives of Christ's character. He says, "You have given yourselves to Me, and I give you to the world. I am the light of the world; I present you to the world as My representatives." As Christ in the fullest sense represents the Father, so we are to represent Christ. Let none of those who name the name of Christ be cowards in His cause. For Christ's sake stand as if looking within the open portals of the city of God.

Ellen G. White
Battle Creek, Michigan
March 20, 1891

Part 1

The Review and Herald Articles

Chapter 1

Work Among the Colored People

I have a most earnest interest in the work to be done among the colored people. This is a branch of work that has been strangely neglected. The reason that this large class of human beings, who have souls to save or to lose, have been so long neglected, is the prejudice that the white people have felt and manifested against mingling with them in religious worship. They have been despised, shunned, and treated with abhorrence, as though crime were upon them, when they were helpless and in need, when men should have labored most earnestly for their salvation. They have been treated without pity. The priests and the Levites have looked upon their wretchedness, and have passed by on the other side.

What should be done for the colored race has long been a vexed question, because professed Christians have not had the Spirit of Christ. They have been called by His name but they have not imitated His example. Men have thought it necessary to plan in such a way as to meet the prejudice of the white people; and a wall of separation in religious worship has been built up between the colored people and the white people.

The white people have declared themselves willing that the colored people should be converted. They have no objection to this. They were willing that they should be grafted into the same parent stock, Christ, and become branches with themselves of the living Vine; yet they were not willing to sit by the side of their colored brethren and sing and pray and bear witness to the truth which they had in common. Not for a moment could they tolerate the idea that they should together bear the fruit that should be found on the Christian tree. The image of Christ might be stamped upon the soul, but it still would be necessary to have a separate church and a separate service. But the question is, Is this in harmony with the moving of the Spirit of God? Is it not after the manner in which the Jewish people acted in the days of Christ? Is not this prejudice against the colored people on the part of the white people similar to that which was cherished by the Jews against the Gentiles? They cultivated the idea until it became deep-rooted that the Gentile should not share the privileges of light and truth that were given to the Jews. They believed that the Jews alone should be recipients of heavenly grace and favor. Christ worked throughout His life to break down this prejudice. No human power alone could overcome it. This prejudice was created not by mere flesh and blood, but by principalities and powers; and in wrestling against it He was wrestling against the rulers of the darkness of this world, against spiritual wickedness in high places.

Again and again men have devised plans whereby to keep up the line of separation and still bring the colored race within the influence of the gospel; but the Lord has blown upon the effort, and made it of none effect. The inquiry among us may be, "What shall we do?" "Wherefore take unto you the whole armor of God, that ye may be able to withstand in the evil day, and having done all, to stand. Stand therefore, having your loins girt about with truth, and having on the breastplate of righteousness; and your feet shod with the preparation of the gospel of peace; above all, taking the shield of faith, wherewith ye shall be able to quench all the fiery darts of the wicked. And take the helmet of salvation, and the sword of the Spirit, which is the word of God."

We should take into consideration the fact that efforts are being made at great expense to send the gospel to the darkened regions of the world, to enlighten the savage inhabitants of the islands of the sea, to bring instruction to the ignorant and idolatrous; yet here in the very midst of us are millions of people who are practically heathen, who have souls to save or to lose, and yet they are set aside and passed by as was the wounded man by the priest and the Levite. Professedly Christian people are leaving them to perish in their sins.

There are two classes in our world. The Lord has sent out the message to those who are represented by the first class, who have had great privileges and opportunities, who have had great light and innumerable blessings. They have been entrusted by the Lord with the living oracles. They are represented by the class to whom the king sent an invitation to the marriage feast. Jesus said, "The kingdom of heaven is like unto a certain king, which made a marriage for his son, and sent forth his servants to call them that are bidden to the wedding: and they would not come. Again, he sent forth other servants, saying, Tell them which are bidden, Behold, I have prepared my dinner: my oxen and my fatlings are killed, and all things are ready: come unto the marriage. But they made light of it, and went their ways, one to his farm, another to his merchandise: and the remnant took his servants, and entreated them spitefully, and slew them. But when the king heard thereof, he was wroth: and he sent forth his armies, and destroyed those murderers, and burned up their city."

Then saith he to his servants, "The wedding is ready, but they which were bidden were not worthy. Go ye therefore into the highways, and as many as ye shall find, bid to the marriage. So those servants went out into the highways, and gathered together all as many as they found, both bad and good: and the wedding was furnished with guests."

How few respond to the gracious invitation of Heaven. Christ is insulted when His messages are despised and His gracious, winning, liberal invitation is rejected. Those that were bidden to the marriage feast at first, began to make excuses. They allowed minor things to occupy their attention, and lost their eternal interests out of their reckoning. While some made temporal interests their excuse, and were totally indifferent toward the messages and messengers, others manifested a spirit of determined hatred, and took the Lord's servants and entreated them spitefully and slew them. A power from beneath moved upon human agencies who were not under the direct influence of the Holy Spirit.

There are two distinct classes—those who are saved through faith in Christ and through obedience to His law, and those who refuse the truth as it is in Jesus. It will be impossible for those who refuse Christ through the period of probation to become justified after the record of their lives has passed into eternity. Now is the time to work for the salvation of men, for probation still continues.

Let national and denominational distinctions be laid aside. Caste and rank are not recognized by God and should not be by His workers. Those who esteem themselves superior to their fellow men on account of position or property are exalting themselves above their fellow men, but they are esteemed by the universe of Heaven as the lowest of all. Let us take a lesson from the words of inspiration that reprove us for this spirit, and also give us great encouragement: "Thus saith the Lord, Let not the wise man glory in his wisdom, neither let the mighty man glory in his might, let not the rich man glory in his riches: but let him that glorieth glory in this, that he understandeth and knoweth me, that I am the Lord which exercise lovingkindness, judgment, and righteousness, in the earth: for in these things I delight, saith the Lord."

No human mind should seek to draw the line between the colored and white people. Let circumstances indicate what shall be done, for the Lord has His hand on the lever of circumstances. As the truth is brought to bear upon the minds of both colored and white people, as souls are thoroughly converted, they will become new men and women in Christ Jesus. Christ says, "A new heart also will I give you," and that new heart bears the divine image. Those who are converted among the white people will experience a change in their sentiments. The prejudice which they have inherited and cultivated toward the colored race will die away. They will realize that there is no respect of persons with God. Those who are converted among the colored race will be cleansed from sin, will wear the white robe of Christ's righteousness, which has been woven in the loom of heaven. Both white and colored people must enter into the path of obedience through the same way.

The test will come, not as regards the outward complexion, but as regards the condition of the heart. Both the white and the colored people have the same Redeemer, who has paid the ransom money with His own life for every member of the human family. If those to whom Christ first sends His invitation to the marriage supper refuse to receive the message, He will send His messengers into the highways and hedges to compel the people to come in, by means of a message so full of the light of Heaven that they will not dare to refuse. The gospel was first to be brought to those to whom God had entrusted precious truths that He desired they should make known to others. He entrusted to them the responsibility of imparting the knowledge of God and of Jesus Christ whom He had sent. The Lord wrought wondrously for the children of Israel. He finally sent to them His own Son, the Prince of life, the Messiah, to whom all their sacrifices and offerings pointed; but they would not receive Him. They rejected the message He bore. They refused the Messiah in whom their hope centered; but when they refused to hear the messages, rejecting the invitation that He gave, the Lord turned to the Gentile world.

Those who ought to have known God and Jesus Christ whom He had sent, who ought to have united with the Sent of God in giving the message to the heathen world, would not themselves receive the invitation, and could not therefore say to others, Come, for all things are now ready. The disciples of Christ were commissioned to proclaim the message of mercy to those in the highways and the byways of the Lord's great moral vineyard. "And the Spirit and the bride say, Come. And let him that heareth {believeth} say, Come. And let him that is athirst come. And whosoever will, let him take the water of life freely."

The Lord has a work that must be done, not only for those who are in the highways and the byways, but for those in high positions of trust. Divine power is promised, not to those who are strongest, but to those who are weakest.

Those who are accounted the strongest and the most enlightened should go to the aid of those who are in most need of help and enlightenment. Everyone can become a laborer together with God, working with Him for the salvation of the souls of the colored race.

It was when Moses stood before God, conscious of his inefficiency, that he was in the very condition in which the Lord could best reveal to him His saving grace. When he had become weak, Christ could reveal to him His power and majesty. The Lord could do little through him when he was the general of armies. He knew that he was the chosen of God, and that he would do a great and special work in delivering the Hebrew nation from bondage; but he sought to do his work in his own way, trusting in his zeal and violence.

The Lord did not propose to do the work in this way. For forty years Moses was placed in the wilderness, to learn in the school of poverty, to learn in the walks of humble life, that he was weak, inefficient, helpless. He left the court of Egypt with a full knowledge of its fascinations, and had to come down to the simplicity of pastoral life. As a shepherd, it was necessary for him to look after the flock, to leave the ninety and nine in the valley and to go in search of the wandering sheep. He had to climb the mountain steep, to search through the tangled brushwood, to look over the precipices, that he might find the lost.

One day he saw a bush ablaze on the mountain, and stood wondering because the bush was not consumed. As he was gazing in astonishment, he heard a voice that seemed to come from the very center of the flame, saying, "Moses, Moses. And he said, Here am I. And he said, Draw not nigh hither: put off thy shoes from off thy feet, for the place whereon thou standest is holy ground. Moreover he said, I am the God of thy father, the God of Abraham, the God of Isaac, and the God of Jacob. And Moses hid his face; for he was afraid to look upon God." Then the Lord gave Moses his commission, sending him to deliver Israel, the lost sheep of Israel in Egypt. Moses pleaded that he was inefficient, that Pharaoh would not believe his message nor hearken to his voice.

He pleaded that the Hebrews themselves would not hearken to him, and would question the fact that the Lord had appeared to him. But the Lord said, "Certainly I will be with thee." "And the Lord said unto him, What is that in thine hand? And he said, A rod. And he said, Cast it on the ground. And he cast it on the ground, and it became a serpent; and Moses fled from before it. And the Lord said unto Moses, Put forth thine hand, and take it by the tail. And he put forth his hand, and caught it, and it became a rod in his hand." The Lord revealed to him the fact that he could manifest such signs and miracles as would convince his people of the divine authority of the message and of the messenger that he sent. The Lord can do wonders, even with the simplest instrumentalities.

Every one whom the Lord calls should be distrustful of self, and have full trust in God. Moses went forth in the name of *"I am that I am,"* without outward display of grandeur; yet the rod in his hand was a symbol of the divine power of Jehovah, and Moses was the instrumentality through whom God would deliver Israel from the bondage of tyranny. There is a work that must be done now by the children of God. For long years the colored race has been neglected, has been left in the slavery of sin, and they are as sheep that have no shepherd. Long ago much might have been done that has not been done. As a people we should do more for the colored race in America than we have yet done. In the work we shall need to move with carefulness, being endowed with wisdom from above. (*The Review and Herald,* April 2, 1895)

Chapter 2

An Appeal for the Southern Field

Dear Brethren and Sisters in America:

I would appeal to you on behalf of the Southern field. If we consulted our own ease and pleasure, we would not desire to enter this field; but we are not to consult our own ease. "Even Christ pleased not himself"; but we are to consider the fact that that field is no more discouraging to those who would be laborers together with God than was the field of the world as it presented itself before the only-begotten Son of God. When He came to earth to seek and to save that which was lost, He did not consult His own ease or pleasure. He left His high command, He laid aside His heavenly honor and glory, He laid off His glorious diadem and royal robe, and left the royal courts, in order that He might come to earth to save fallen man.

Though He possessed eternal riches, yet for our sakes He became poor, that He might enrich the human race. By accepting the Son of God as their Redeemer, by exercising faith in Him, the sons and the daughters of Adam may become heirs of God and joint heirs with Jesus Christ. The apostle says: "Ye know the grace of our Lord Jesus Christ, that, though he was rich, yet for your sakes he became poor, that ye through his poverty might be rich."

Christ was willing to come to a world that was all marred and seared with the curse—the result of Adam's transgression of the law of God.

He was willing to undertake the case of fallen beings who had lost their original holiness, and who were in ignorance of the perfection of God's character. He was willing to come to bring back to loyalty those who were not subject to God's moral government. In the grand counsels of Heaven it was found that it was positively necessary that there should be a revelation of God to man in the person of His only-begotten Son. He came to earth to be "the true Light, which lighteth every man that cometh into the world."

The Southern field is beset with difficulties, and should I present the field to you as it has been presented to me, many of you would draw back and say, "No, I cannot enter such a field." But the condition of the colored race is no more disheartening than was the condition of the world when Christ left heaven to work for fallen man. He clothed His divinity with humanity, and came into the world, in order that His humanity might touch humanity and His divinity lay hold upon the throne of God in man's behalf. He came to seek the one lost sheep, to bring back the wandering one from the wilderness of sin to the heavenly fold. He was treated with every indignity by those whom He came to save from eternal ruin, and the missionary to the Southern field will need to arm himself with the mind that was in Christ Jesus. The record says: "He came unto his own, and his own received him not. But as many as received him, to them gave he power to become the sons of God, even to them that believe on his name."

The Southern race has been neglected. Men have passed by on the other side, as the priest and the Levite passed by the wounded, robbed, bruised, and beaten one. But a certain Samaritan, as he journeyed that way, not only saw him, but he had compassion on him, and went to him, and bound up his wounds, set him on his own beast, brought him to an inn, and took care of him. How many have left the colored race to perish by the wayside? Since the slaves gained their freedom at terrible loss of life both to the North and to the South, they have been greatly neglected by those who professed to know God, and as a result thousands of them have failed to gain spiritual freedom. But shall this indifference continue? Shall not decided efforts be made to save them? Sin has degraded and corrupted the human family, but Christ did not leave men to perish in their degradation. He who was one with the Father came to our world to bridge the gulf that sin had made, which separated man from God because of transgression.

Christ, the brightness of His Father's glory, beheld humanity in its wretchedness and sinfulness, beheld souls tainted with corruption, depraved and deformed. He knew that the fallen race tended more to evil than to good, and practiced the most hateful vices. The heavenly hosts looked upon the world as undeserving of the sympathy and love of God.

Angels marveled that Christ should undertake to save man in his lost, and as it seemed to them, hopeless condition. They marveled that God could tolerate a race so foul with sin as to be a blot upon His creation. They could see no room for love, but Christ saw that souls must perish unless an arm strong to deliver was reached forth to save.

Satan is the destroyer, but Christ is the restorer. From the first it was Satan's purpose to cause men to transgress the law of God. He misrepresented the character of the Father, trampled upon His law, and cast contempt upon His precepts. He inspired men with his own spirit, and made them partakers of his own attributes, and caused them to transgress the law of God. When he had accomplished his work of ruin, he pointed to the degraded, sin-polluted souls whom he had made subject to a thousand vices, and declared that they were too degraded, too wretched, to be redeemed by Heaven. He sought to present mankind in the most discouraging aspect, so that reformation might seem hopeless.

Though he could not prevail with his temptations in assailing Christ, or cause Him to fail or be discouraged, yet he often succeeds too well with those who should be laborers together with God. But his plans to cause the work to cease are not wholly successful. Through the grace of God those whom the enemy has oppressed for generations, rise up to the dignity of God-given manhood and womanhood and present themselves as sons and daughters of the Most High. This result is generally brought about through well-directed, persevering missionary labor.

Why should not Seventh-day Adventists become true laborers together with God in seeking to save the souls of the colored race? Instead of a few, why should not many go forth to labor in this long-neglected field? Where are the families who will become missionaries and who will engage in labor in this field? Where are the men who have means and experience so that they can go forth to these people and work for them just where they are? There are men who can educate them in agricultural lines, who can teach the colored people to sow seed and plant orchards.

There are others who can teach them to read, and can give them an object lesson from their own life and example. Show them what you yourself can do to gain a livelihood, and it will be an education to them. Are we not called upon to do this very work? Are there not many who need to learn to love God supremely and their fellow men as themselves? In the Southern field are many thousands of people who have souls to save or to lose. Are there not many among those who claim to believe the truth who will go forth into this field to do the work for which Christ gave up His ease, His riches, and His life?

Christ gave up all in order that He might bring salvation to every people, nation, and tongue. He bridged the gulf that sin had made, in order that through His merits man might be reconciled to God. Why is there not an army of workers enlisted under the bloodstained banner of Prince Emmanuel, ready to go forth to enlighten those who are ignorant and depraved? Why do we not go forth to bring souls out of darkness into light? Why do we not teach the perishing to believe in Christ as their personal Savior, and aid them to see Christ by faith, and wash in the fountain that has been opened to cleanse away the sins of the world?

We should teach those who are filthy how to cast away their old, sin-stained garments of character, and how to put on Christ's righteousness. We should plant in their darkened minds the elevating, ennobling thoughts of heavenly things. By faith, by Christlike sympathy and example, we should lead the polluted into pure and holy lives. We should live such a life before them that they will discern the difference between error and vice, and purity, righteousness, and holiness. We should make straight paths for our feet, lest the lame be turned out of the way.

Many who claim to be Christians have accomplished little in the world because they have not kept their eyes upon Jesus, and have permitted iniquity to overcome them. Many who have gone forth as missionaries have fallen into sin, and Satan has exulted because men who claimed to be workers together with God were not daily converted, and were not, by looking unto Jesus, transformed in character. They did not make God their strength, and so made crooked paths for their feet. They could not bring the poor, ignorant souls who were debased by sin into a new life, even into the life of God, because their own life was not hid with Christ in God.

As workers together with God, we must yoke up with Jesus Christ, and put on Christ. When we are planted in Him, we shall grow in likeness of Christ's character. We are to be living epistles, and men are to read in our lives what it means to be a Christian. We are to represent Christ in character, and self is to be hidden with Christ in God. When this is our experience, we shall find that the angels of God will cooperate with us. Feeling our dependence upon God, we shall realize the force of Christ's words when He said, "Without me ye can do nothing." We shall then know how to have sympathy for the neglected, the oppressed, the despised, and yet at the same time have no sympathy with degradation, but in the midst of sin press closer and closer to the side of Jesus. We shall be grieved and shocked at the sins which are committed while we wear the yoke with Christ and are preparing to be temples for the indwelling of the Holy Ghost.

Men who have faith and hope and love are partakers of the divine nature and have overcome the corruption that is in the world through lust. Such men are successful workers; for they build upon the sure foundation, gold, silver, and precious stones. They build with goodly material which is most valuable. They do not build with that which is perishable, with that which is compared to wood, hay, and stubble, which will be burned up in the fires of the last days. Their work results in redeeming souls that shall stand before the throne of God.

Christ said to His disciples: "They that be whole need not a physician, but they that are sick. . . . I am not come to call the righteous, but sinners to repentance." Those who realize their guilt, feel their need of the Savior. Why, O why, has not more been done to diffuse light into the darkened minds of the colored race? Christ died for the colored people as verily as He died for the white people.

Through faith in Christ the colored people may attain unto eternal life as verily as may the white people. Those whom the Lord sees neglected by us have been entrusted with reasoning powers, and yet they have been treated as though they had no souls. They have been wounded by a so-called Christian nation. They have been left by the wayside, and decided efforts will have to be made to counteract the wrong that has been done them. But though they have been despised and neglected of men, God has given special help and enlightenment to many who were in slavery. He has illuminated their darkness when they were in the most unfavorable circumstances, and they have revealed to the world the elements of the greatness in Christian character.

Many of the black race have been rich in faith and trust in God. They have manifested divine compassion for those whom they could help. They have known what it was to hunger for sympathy and help; for they were but neglected by those who saw their wretchedness and could have helped them, but who passed by on the other side, as the priest and the Levite passed by the bruised and wounded one. There are souls among the colored race that can be reached, and the very kind of labor which their circumstances require should be put forth, that they may be saved. When these souls are converted to the truth, they will become partakers of the divine nature, and will go forth to rescue their fellow men, to lead those who are in darkness into light. They can be helped in their low estate, and in their turn can contribute to the good of others.

But there are many among the colored people whose intellect has been too long darkened to be speedily fitted for fruitfulness in good works. Many are held in bondage to depraved appetite. Many are slaves to debasing passions, and their character is of such an order as will not enable them to be a blessing. Sin and depravity have locked up their senses. They need help as much as the veriest heathen, and unless they have the right kind of help, they will be lost. But they may be taught to know God and Jesus Christ whom He has sent.

The bright beams of the Sun of Righteousness may shine into the darkened chambers of their mind. They need to catch a glimpse of God. It is their privilege to have eternal life, to be in union with God, and it is the privilege of those who know the truth to repeat the story again and again of God's wonderful love to man as manifested on Calvary's cross. The chain that is let down from the throne of God is long enough to reach into the lowest depths of sin. Hold up a sin-pardoning Savior before the lost and lowly, for Jesus has made a divine interposition in their behalf. He is able to reach to the lowest depths and lift them up from the pit of sin, that they may be acknowledged as children of God, heirs with Christ to an immortal inheritance. They may have the life that measures with the life of God. (*The Review and Herald,* November 26, 1895)

Chapter 3

An Appeal for the South (2)

God estimates man not by the circumstances of his birth, not by his position or wealth, not by his advantages in educational lines, but by the price paid for his redemption. Man is of value with God in proportion as he permits the divine image to be retraced upon his soul.

However misshapen has been his character, although he may have been counted as an outcast among men, the man who permits the grace of Christ to enter his soul will be reformed in character and will be raised up from his condition of guilt, degradation, and wretchedness. God has made every provision in order that the lost one may become His child. The frailest human being may be elevated, ennobled, refined, and sanctified by the grace of God. This is the reason God values men; and those who are workers together with God, who are filled with divine compassion, will see and estimate men in the same way that God sees and estimates them.

Whatever may be the nationality or color, whatever may be the social condition, the missionary for God will look upon all men as the purchase of the blood of Christ, and will understand that there is no caste with God. No one is to be looked upon with indifference or to be regarded as unimportant, for every soul has been purchased with an infinite price. Therefore, in the name of Jesus Christ of Nazareth, let not the colored race be longer neglected by those who claim to believe in Christ as the Savior of men. Let not one who claims to have heard the gracious words, "Thy sins be forgiven thee," hold himself aloof from those whose lives have been dark and shadowed.

Was it God's purpose that the colored people should have so much guilt and woe in their lives? No. Men who have had greater advantages than they have had, have taught them immorality, both by precept and example. Debasing practices have been forced upon them, and they have received low conceptions of life, and even their conceptions of the Christian life are of a depraved order. But the people who have been more favorably situated, who have had light and liberty, who have had an opportunity to know God, and Jesus Christ whom He has sent, are responsible for the moral darkness that enshrouds their colored brethren. Can they who have been so highly privileged afford to stand in their pride and importance and feel that they are altogether too good to associate with this depraved race? Let those who profess to be Christians look to the example of Christ. He stooped to take human nature, in order that He might be able to reach man where he was. The Majesty of heaven came to seek and to save that which was lost; and shall those for whom Christ has done so much, stand aloof from their fellow men who are now perishing in their sins?

The Lord invites His people to become workers together with Him in rebuilding and reshaping character according to the true standard of moral rectitude. Through faith in Christ we are to be recreated in His image. Jesus says, Behold, I create a new thing in the earth. Apostate man is to be recovered; fallen humanity is to be elevated; sin is to be pardoned; and sinners are to be saved, that God may be eternally glorified. The treasures of wisdom which have been hidden for ages are to be brought forth for the enriching of the lost. O what treasures of wisdom are to be opened up for the view of the world! Every divine resource is placed at the disposal of man, in order that he may become a colaborer with God. Nothing has been withheld. When God gave His only-begotten Son to our world, He gave all the treasures of heaven. What power, what glory, has been revealed in Christ Jesus! The greatest display of majesty and power is given to the world through the only-begotten Son of God.

With this power at our command, I would ask in the name of Jesus Christ of Nazareth why it is that God's people do not awake to their duty? Why is it that every individual does not become an example in doing the work that the time demands in first giving himself and then his talents of means and ability for the enlightenment and salvation of a people who are in the dense darkness of pitiful and most deplorable ignorance? Are there not men, women, and youth who will go forth to establish schools, and thus become teachers to instruct the colored people so that they may be enabled to read the word of God?

We must teach them to read God's word, or they will become the ready dupes of false shepherds that misinterpret the Scriptures and that manufacture doctrines and teach traditions which will lead them into the paths of perdition There are preachers and teachers among the colored people who are addicted to licentious habits; and how can they understand the binding claims of the law of God when the standard of righteousness is not revealed and exalted before their eyes by the precept and example of their teachers? We must go among them and show them how to honor and obey God's law, in order that they may be prepared to have a part in the new earth.

Are there not those who can go from house to house, from family to family, and who can repeat the ABC of true Christian experience? Let Christ be your text. In all your labor let it be apparent that you know Jesus. Present His purity and saving grace, that by beholding, these people may become changed into the divine image. Among most of the colored people we find unseemly practices in their worship of God. They become much excited, and put forth physical exertions that are uncalled for in the solemn worship of God. Their superstitious ideas and uncomely practices cannot at once be dispelled. We must not combat their ideas and treat them with contempt. But let the worker give them an example of what constitutes true heart-service in religious worship. Let not the colored people be excluded from the religious assemblies of the white people.

They have no chance to exchange their superstitious exercises for a worship that is more sacred and elevating if they are shut out from association with intelligent white people who should give them an example of what they should be and do. Let the white people practice the self-denial necessary, and let them remember that nothing is to be regarded as unimportant which affects the religious life of so vast a number of people as that which composes the colored race. They conduct their worship according to the instruction they have received, and they think that a religion which has no excitement, no noise, no bodily exercises, is not worth the name of religion. These ignorant worshipers need instruction and guidance. They can be won by kindness, and can be confirmed in well-doing. Both old and young will need to be instructed as one would instruct a family of children.

Let the worker give them an example by associating with them and by revealing the virtues of Christ Jesus. They need to be brought in contact with cultivated minds, to come into association with those whose hearts are softened and subdued by the Holy Spirit. They are imitative, and will catch up pure sentiments, and be influenced by elevated aspirations. A new taste will thus be created, and elevated desires will spring up for things that are of good report, pure, honest, and lovely. But if the colored people are left in their present condition, and do not have presented before them a higher standard of Christianity than they now have, their ideas will become more and more confused, and their religious worship more and more demoralized. They have been strangely neglected. Poverty and want are common among them, and very little has been done to relieve their distress. We cannot be surprised that such neglect should result in hardness of heart and in the practice of vice, but God cares for this neglected class.

The colored people have souls to save, and we must enter into the work, and become colaborers with Jesus Christ. We cannot leave them as we have left them in the past. We cannot be justified in expending money so lavishly in providing conveniences for ourselves and in furnishing facilities for those who have been more fortunate, and are already abundantly supplied with every facility, and do nothing for those who know not God and Jesus Christ whom He hath sent. We must not abandon millions of the colored race to their degradation, and because they are degraded, pass them by on the other side.

Let us bear in mind the words that Christ spoke to the people who were honored above others in being privileged to have the Lord Jesus Christ to labor among them, and yet who did not appreciate this privilege and did not diffuse the light of Heaven to others. He said: "Woe unto thee, Chorazin! woe unto thee, Bethsaida! for if the mighty works, which were done in you, had been done in Tyre and Sidon, they would have repented long ago in sackcloth and ashes. But I say unto you, It shall be more tolerable for Tyre and Sidon at the day of judgment, than for you. And thou, Capernaum, which art exalted unto heaven, shalt be brought down to hell: for if the mighty works, which have been done in thee, had been done in Sodom, it would have remained until this day. But I say unto you, That it shall be more tolerable for the land of Sodom in the day of judgment, than for thee."

But while Christ pronounced a woe upon those who did not repent at His preaching, He had a word of encouragement for the lowly: "At that time Jesus answered and said, I thank thee, O Father, Lord of heaven and earth, because thou hast hid these things from the wise and prudent, and hast revealed them unto babes. Even so, Father: for so it seemed good in thy sight."

Many of the colored people are among the lowly who will receive the Word of God, and shall not this long-neglected work of enlightening the colored people be entered into perseveringly, and be carried forward all the more diligently because it has been so long neglected? We must do a work for the colored race that has not yet been done. "God so loved the world, that he gave his only begotten Son, that whosoever believeth in him might not perish, but have everlasting life." The Son of God, the Creator of the world, sacrificed His own life in order that He might become the Redeemer of fallen humanity. He made an infinite sacrifice that He might become man's surety and substitute, and shall we remain indifferent to a downtrodden, abused race?

God cares for the colored people, and if we would cooperate with Him for the salvation of their souls, we must care for them, too, and become laborers together with Him. We need to repent before God, because we have neglected missionary work in the most abandoned part of God's moral vineyard. There needs to be a stirring up among the members of our churches. There needs to be concern created for our colored brethren at the great heart of the work. We should rouse up to the interest that true Christians ought to feel for those who are depressed and morally degraded. The fact that their skin is dark does not prove that they are sinners above the white race. Much of their depravity is the fruit of the neglect of the white people. They have not felt the sympathy that they ought to have felt for the abandoned and wretched. Those who profess to love Christ should have worked for their colored brethren until hope would have sprung up in their hearts.

Many are completely discouraged, and they have become stolid because they have been neglected, despised, and forsaken. The poor and unfortunate are numbered by thousands, and yet we have looked on indifferently, and seen their sorrow, and have passed by on the other side. Their degraded condition is our condemnation. The Christian world are guilty because they have failed to help the very ones who most need help. Christ says, "I am not come to call the righteous, but sinners to repentance."

Should we not work the Southern field? We have had every advantage in temporal and spiritual things, and shall we do nothing for our colored brethren? We cannot abandon the colored race and be accounted as guiltless. Christ speaks of His own mission in these words: "The Spirit of the Lord is upon me, because he hath anointed me to preach the gospel to the poor; he hath sent me to heal the brokenhearted, to preach deliverance to the captives, and recovering of sight to the blind, to set at liberty them that are bruised, to preach the acceptable year of the

Lord." Are we not to follow the example of Christ? Are we not, as His human agents, to carry forward the work He came to do? Christ said, "They that be whole need not a physician, but they that are sick."

We cannot leave souls for whom Christ died to be the prey of Satan's temptations. We cannot abandon this great flock to their ignorance, want, suffering, and corruption. This would not be doing the will of God. We cannot heap advantages upon ourselves and upon those who are not in need and pass by those who are in utter want, and be approved of God. This neglect is charged against those who have had great light, who have had marvelous opportunities, and who yet leave so large a portion of God's moral vineyard unworked. For years Satan has been sowing his tares among the colored people, and the field cannot be worked as easily now as it could have been worked years ago. But there should be no delay now.

Reproach is brought upon Jesus Christ when those who profess to be carrying the last message of mercy to the world pass this field by. Christ did not pass by the needy and suffering. He united works of mercy with the message of salvation He came to bear to men. He engaged in a constant, untiring ministry, and worked for the perishing and sorrowful. He prefaced His message of love by deeds of ministry and beneficence, leaving us an example that we should follow in His steps. (*The Review and Herald,* December 3, 1895)

Chapter 4

An Appeal for the South (3)

The World's Redeemer clearly defines what our duty is. To the lawyer who asked Him how he should obtain eternal life, He said: "What is written in the law? how readest thou? And he answering said, Thou shalt love the Lord thy God with all thy heart, and with all thy soul, and with all thy strength, and with all thy mind; and thy neighbor as thyself. And he said unto him, Thou hast answered right: this do, and thou shalt live. But he, willing to justify himself, said unto Jesus, And who is my neighbor?" Then Jesus related the parable of the good Samaritan, and clearly showed that he is our neighbor who most needs our charity and help.

We are to practice the commandments of God, and stand true to the relation which God has designed shall exist between man and his fellow man. It was never God's purpose that society should be separated into classes, that there should be an alienation between the rich and the poor, the high and the low, the learned and the unlearned. But the practice of separating society into distinct circles is becoming more and more decided. God designed that those to whom He entrusted talents of means, ability, and gifts of grace, should be good stewards of His beneficence, and not seek to reap all the advantages for themselves. God does not estimate man by the amount of wealth, talent, or education that he may have. He values man in proportion as he becomes a good steward of His mercy and love.

Those who center everything upon themselves misinterpret the character of God. The Lord designed that the gifts He bestows upon men should be used to minister to the unfortunate and the suffering ones among humanity.

We are in God's world, and are handling His goods, and we shall be called upon to render a strict account of the use that we have made of His entrusted riches. If we have hoarded God's gifts for our own advantage, if we have indulged in luxury, if we have heaped up treasure for ourselves, and have been indifferent to the wants of those who are suffering around us, we shall be charged as guilty of embezzling God's goods.

The cries of suffering humanity go up to God, and He hears their complaints of hunger, of ignorance, and of darkness. He will surely judge those who neglect His purchased possession, who leave the suffering to perish when it is in their power to relieve them. He will hold us accountable for the guilt of those who are left to be the sport of Satan's temptations, and who in their ignorance and blindness charge God with dealing partially with the human race. It is because the rich neglect to do the work for the poor that God designed they should do, that they grow more proud, more self-sufficient, more self-indulgent and hardhearted. They separate the poor from them simply because they are poor, and thus give them occasion to become envious and jealous. Many become bitter, and are imbued with hatred toward those who have everything when they have nothing.

God weighs actions, and every one who has been unfaithful in his stewardship, who has failed to remedy evils which it was in his power to remedy, will be of no esteem in the courts of heaven. Those who are indifferent to the wants of the needy will be counted unfaithful stewards, and will be registered as enemies of God and man. Those who misappropriate the means that God has entrusted to them to help the very ones who need their help, prove that they have no connection with Christ, because they fail to manifest the tenderness of Christ toward those who are less fortunate than themselves.

As Christians, we are to manifest to the world the character of Christ in all the affairs of life. To be a Christian means to act in Christ's stead, to represent Christ. We are not to seek to get rid of the responsibilities that connect us with our fellow men. God has not placed us in the world simply to please and honor and glorify ourselves. The character of our Christianity is tested by the dependent ones who are around us, who are ignorant and helpless. It is not proper to pile building upon building in localities where there are abundant facilities, and neglect fields that are nigh and afar off, where there is need of starting missionary enterprises. Instead of closing our eyes and senses to the wants of those who have nothing, instead of adding more and more facilities to those that are already abundant, let us seek to see what we can do to relieve the distresses of the poor, bruised souls of the colored people.

Those who are heaping advantages upon advantages where there are already more than ample facilities, are not doing a work that will strengthen men in spirituality; and for neglecting destitute fields they are weighed in the balances of the sanctuary and are found wanting. The Lord has given abundant light upon the subject of diffusing the knowledge of the truth, and no one is justified in following a selfish course. Those to whom God has entrusted much, who command the largest resources in doing a good work in behalf of the needy, and who yet have failed to do it, have withdrawn themselves from their own flesh, and have neglected their ministry to God's purchased possession, in order to gratify their own inclination.

How does God look upon those who have left the poor to their poverty, the ignorant to their darkness and ignorance? How does He regard those who are willing to let the lost remain the slaves of circumstances which could have been changed in such a way as to bring relief to the distressed? God calls upon men to become Bible Christians, to represent the example given them by Christ. Who can tell what will be the result of a self-denying, cross-bearing life? Eternity will reveal the result of following Jesus, and all will be amazed at the fruit that will be made manifest.

We need men who will become leaders in home and foreign missionary enterprises. We need men whose sympathies are not congealed, but whose hearts go out to the perishing that are nigh and afar off. The ice that binds about souls that are frozen up with selfishness needs to be melted away, so that every brother shall realize that he is his brother's keeper. Then everyone will go forth to help his neighbor to see the truth and to serve God in an acceptable service.

Then those who profess the name of Christ will aid others in the formation of a Christlike character. If everyone would work in Christ's lines, much would be done to change the condition that now exists among the poor and distressed. Pure religion and undefiled would gleam forth as a bright and shining light. God's love in the heart would melt away the barriers of race and caste and would remove the obstacles with which men have barred others away from the truth as it is in Jesus. True religion will induce its advocates to go forth into the highways and byways of life. It will lead them to help the suffering, and enable them to be faithful shepherds going forth into the wilderness to seek and to save the lost, to lead back the perishing sheep and lambs.

The most unfortunate may bear the image of God, and they are of value to God. Those who have true religion will realize that it is their supreme duty to reveal Christ to men, to make manifest the fact that they have learned in the school of Christ. O that we might individually realize that we are simply stewards in trust of God's means, and that we are to use the gifts God has given us as Christ used His eternal riches in seeking and saving that which is lost. We are only trustees, only stewards, and by and by we must give a reckoning to the Master. He will inquire how we have used His goods, and whether or not we have ministered to His family in the world. If we have enjoyed the comforts and blessings of life, and have had no care for those who were less fortunate, and have failed to relieve those who were needy and suffering, for whom Christ has given His life, we shall not hear the words of approval, "Well done, thou good and faithful servant."

If God has entrusted to us the precious light of truth, and has given us a knowledge of Jesus Christ whom He has sent, and we have failed to diffuse that light, we shall be confronted with the souls whom we have held in darkness in the great day of God. We shall be dealt with as we have dealt with others. The King will say to those on His right hand: "Come, ye blessed of my Father, inherit the kingdom prepared for you from the foundation of the world: for I was an hungred, and ye gave me meat: I was thirsty, and ye gave me drink: I was a stranger, and ye took me in: naked, and ye clothed me: I was sick, and ye visited me: I was in prison, and ye came unto me. Then shall the righteous answer him, saying, Lord, when saw we thee an hungred, and fed thee? or thirsty, and gave thee drink? When saw we thee a stranger, and took thee in? or naked, and clothed thee? Or when saw we thee sick, or in prison, and came unto thee? And the King shall answer and say unto them, Verily I say unto you, Inasmuch as ye have done it unto one of the least of these my brethren, ye have done it unto me." (*The Review and Herald*, December 19, 1895)

Chapter 5

An Example in History

The Hebrew nation were in servitude for a great number of years. They were slaves in Egypt, and the Egyptians treated them as though they had a right to control them in soul, body, and spirit. But the Lord was not indifferent to their condition, He had not forgotten His oppressed people. The record says: "God heard their groaning, and God remembered his covenant with Abraham, Isaac, and with Jacob. And God looked upon the children of Israel, and God had respect unto them." "The Lord said, I have surely seen the affliction of my people which are in Egypt, and have heard their cry by reason of their taskmasters; for I know their sorrows; and I am come down to deliver them out of the hand of the Egyptians, and to bring them up out of that land unto a good land and a large, unto a land flowing with milk and honey."

When God called Moses to be His instrument in delivering the Hebrew nation out of cruel bondage, Moses considered the difficulties of the situation, and thought of the obstacles that he would have to encounter in doing this great work. He knew that the people were in blindness and ignorance, that their minds had become beclouded in faith, and that they were almost destitute of a knowledge of God. They had become degraded by associating with a nation of idolaters, and had corrupted their ways by practicing idolatry. Yet there were many who were righteous and steadfast among this downtrodden people. The Lord directed Moses to give them a message from Himself. He said: "Wherefore say unto the children of Israel, I am the Lord, and I will bring you out from under the burdens of the Egyptians, and I will rid you out of their bondage, and I will redeem you with a stretched out arm, and with great judgments: and I will take you to me for a people, and I will be to you a God: and ye shall know that I am the Lord your God, which bringeth you out from under the burdens of the Egyptians."

This nation of slaves was to be taught of God. Jesus Christ, enshrouded in the pillar of cloud and fire, was to be their invisible leader, the ruler over all their tribes. Moses was to be the mouthpiece of God. For forty years God ruled over them as they journeyed through the wilderness.

But the Hebrew nation is not the only nation that has been in cruel bondage, and whose groanings have come to the ears of the Lord of hosts. The Lord God of Israel has looked upon the vast number of human beings who were held in slavery in the United States of America. The United States has been a refuge for the oppressed. It has been spoken of as the bulwark of religious liberty. God has done more for this country than for any other country upon which the sun shines. It has been marvelously preserved from war and bloodshed.

God saw the foul blot of slavery upon this land, He marked the sufferings that were endured by the colored people. He moved upon the hearts of men to work in behalf of those who were so cruelly oppressed. The Southern States became one terrible battlefield. The graves of American sons who had enlisted to deliver the oppressed race are thick in its soil. Many fell in death, giving their lives to proclaim liberty to the captives and the opening of the prison to them that were bound. God spoke concerning the captivity of the colored people as verily as He did concerning the Hebrew captives, and said: "I have surely seen the affliction of my people . . . , and have heard their cry by reason of their taskmasters; for I know their sorrows; and I am come down to deliver them."

The Lord wrought in freeing the Southern slaves; but He designed to work still further for them as He did for the children of Israel, whom He took forth to educate, to refine, and ennoble. Christ Himself wrought with His appointed leaders, and directed them as to what they should do for His people that had become so terribly degraded. They were to be kept separate from all nations, to be directed and counseled until, through a correct representation of the divine character, they should come to know God, to reverence and obey His commandments.

Those who study the history of the Israelites should also consider the history of the slaves in America, who have suffered, who have been educated in crime, degraded, and oppressed, and left in ignorance to perish. Their physical freedom was obtained at a great loss of life, and Christians generally should have looked with compassion upon the colored race, for which God had a care. They should have done a work for them that would have uplifted them. They should have worked through the wisdom of God to educate and train them. We have been very neglectful of our colored brethren, and are not yet prepared for the coming of our Lord.

The cries of these neglected people have come up before God. Who has entered into the work since their deliverance from bondage, to teach them the knowledge of God? The condition of the colored people is no more helpless than was the condition of the Hebrew slaves. The children of Israel were addicted to licentiousness, idolatry, gluttony, and gross vices. This is ever the result of slavery. But the Lord looked upon His people, and after their deliverance He educated them. They were not left uncared for. Though they had lost in years of bondage the knowledge of the true God and of His holy law, yet God again revealed Himself to them. In terrible grandeur and awful majesty He proclaimed to them His holy precepts, and commanded them to obey His law.

The Ten Commandments are a transcript of the divine character, and are as unchangeable as the eternal throne. But since the slaves of the South attained to freedom, what have we as Christians done to bear any comparison to what was done for them by those who poured out their lives on the battlefield? Have we not looked upon the difficulties that presented themselves, and drawn back from the work? Perhaps some of us have felt sad over their wretchedness, but what have we done to save them from the slavery of sin? Who have taken hold of this work intelligently? Who have taken upon them the burden of presenting to them spiritual freedom that has been purchased for them at an infinite price? Have we not left them beaten, bruised, despised, and forsaken by the way? Is this the example that God has given us in the history of the deliverance of the children of Israel? By no means.

Walls of separation have been built up between the whites and the blacks. These walls of prejudice will tumble down of themselves as did the walls of Jericho, when Christians obey the Word of God, which enjoins on them supreme love to their Maker and impartial love to their neighbors. For Christ's sake, let us do something now. Let every church whose members claim to believe the truth for this time, look at this neglected, downtrodden race, that, as a result of slavery, have been deprived of the privilege of thinking and acting for themselves. They have been kept at work in the cotton fields, have been driven before the lash like brute beasts, and their children have received no enviable heritage. Many of the slaves had noble minds, but the fact that their skin was dark, was sufficient reason for the whites to treat them as though they were beasts.

When freedom was proclaimed to the captives, a favorable time was given in which to establish schools and to teach the people to take care of themselves. Much of this kind of work was done by various denominations, and God honored their work. Those who attempted to work for the black race had to suffer persecution, and many were martyrs to the cause. It was difficult to educate these people in correct ideas, because they had been compelled to do according to the word of their human masters. They had been subject to human passions, their minds and bodies had been abused, and it was very hard to efface the education of these people and to lead them to change their practices. But these missionaries persevered in their work. They knew that the black man had not chosen his color or his condition and that Christ had died for him as verily as He had died for his white brother. To show sympathy for the released slaves was to expose one's self to ridicule, hatred, and persecution. Old-time prejudice still exists, and those who labor in behalf of the colored race will have to encounter difficulties.

The neglect of the colored race by the American nation is charged against them. Those who claim to be Christians have a work to do in teaching them to read and to follow various trades and engage in different business enterprises. Many among this race have noble traits of character and keen perception of mind. If they had an opportunity to develop, they would stand upon an equality with the whites. The Hebrew nation were educated during their journeying through the wilderness. They engaged in physical and mental labor. They used their muscles in various lines of work.

The history of the wilderness life of God's chosen people was chronicled for the benefit of the Israel of God till the close of time. The apostle says, "Now all these things happened unto them for ensamples: and they are written for our admonition, upon whom the ends of the world are come." The Lord did not forsake His people in their wanderings through the wilderness, but many of them forsook the Lord. The education they had had in Egypt made them subject to temptation, to idolatry, and to licentiousness, and because they disregarded the commandments of the Lord, nearly all the adults who left Egypt were overthrown in the wilderness; but their children were permitted to enter Canaan.

The land of Egypt was nearly desolated to bring freedom to the children of Israel; the Southern States were nearly ruined to bring freedom to the colored race. For four years war was carried on, and many lives were sacrificed, and there is mourning today because of broken family circles.

Unspeakable outrages have been committed against the colored race. They had lived on through years of bondage with no hope of deliverance, and there stretched out before them a dark and dismal future.

They thought that it was their lot to live on under cruel oppression, to yield their bodies and souls to the dominance of man. After their deliverance from captivity how earnestly should every Christian have cooperated with heavenly intelligences who were working for the deliverance of the downtrodden race.

We should have sent missionaries into this field to teach the ignorant. We should have issued books in so simple a style that a child might have understood them, for many of them are only children in understanding. Pictures and object lessons should have been used to present to the mind valuable ideas. Children and youth should have been educated in such a way that they could have been instructors and missionaries to their parents.

Let us prayerfully consider the colored race, and realize that these people are a portion of the purchased possession of Jesus Christ. One of infinite dignity, who was equal with God, humbled Himself so that He might meet man in his fallen, helpless condition, and become an advocate before the Father in behalf of humanity. Jesus did not simply declare His good will toward perishing man, but humbled Himself, taking upon Himself the nature of man. For our sakes He became poor, that we might come into possession of an immortal inheritance, be heirs of God and joint heirs with Jesus Christ. (*The Review and Herald*, December 17, 1895)

Chapter 6

The Bible and the Colored People

The Bible is the most precious book in the world. It is the only guide to direct the soul to the paradise of God. The apostle says: "All scripture is given by inspiration of God, and is profitable for doctrine, for reproof, for correction, for instruction in righteousness: that the man of God may be perfect, throughly furnished unto all good works." The Bible is a precious treasure. It should be in every home, not to be laid away or put upon a shelf, but to be diligently studied. The Bible is the hope of both the white and the colored race. The idea is disseminated that common people should not study the Bible for themselves, but that the minister or teacher should decide all matters of doctrine for them. This is the doctrine that is taught to the colored people; but the Bible is the poor man's book, and all classes of people are to search the Scriptures for themselves. God has given reasoning powers to men, and by bringing our mental faculties into connection with the Word of God, the spiritual powers are awakened, and common people, as well as teachers and clergymen, may understand the will of God.

Christ said to the people, "Search the scriptures; for in them ye think ye have eternal life: and they are they which testify of me." Many of the colored people are unable to read, and as it is necessary to understand the Word of God, it is necessary to teach these people to read. During the days of slavery the colored people were not generally taught to read, because through this accomplishment they became more fully awake to the degradation of their condition. In attaining knowledge, their desire was increased to have liberty, that they might still further pursue their search for knowledge. They saw that it was their right to be subject to no man, but to obey God only. The proclamation that freed the slaves in the Southern States, opened a field into which Christlike workers should have entered to teach those who were hungering and thirsting for knowledge, that they might know God and Jesus Christ whom He has sent. There were precious jewels of truth that should have been searched for as a man would search for hidden treasure.

The Lord has given the Bible to us, and it is our privilege to read it for ourselves. It is our duty to search it diligently, that we may receive more and more light from its sacred pages. As we search the Bible to comprehend the truths of salvation, angels of God are present to strengthen the mind and to aid us in understanding that which will be a benefit to us and to others. We are to explore the sacred volume as a miner explores the veins of ore in the earth, and finds the precious seams of gold. While time shall last, we shall desire to know what the Bible has to say in regard to our relation to Jesus Christ, our responsibility to God as free moral agents. We must search the Scriptures, so that we may know how to accept our responsibilities and how to impart the knowledge we have gained to others who are in need of comfort and hope. We must know by experience what it is to have Christ for our sin bearer, in order that we may intelligently say to others, "Behold the Lamb of God, which taketh away the sin of the world!"

The opinions we have received through listening to the traditions of men must not be permitted to bar the way so that we shall not receive the light that requires reformation and transformation. Enter your closets with the Bible in your hand, and there commune with God, having an ear to hear what the Spirit saith unto you. Let your heart be humbled and teachable, softened and subdued by the Holy Spirit. If you find that your former views are not sustained by the Bible, it is for your eternal interest to learn this as soon as possible; for when God speaks in His Word, our preconceived opinions must be yielded up and our ideas brought into harmony with a "Thus saith the Lord." Christ said, "Sanctify them through thy truth; thy word is truth." With submissive spirit you are to obey the truth at any cost, knowing that the precepts of the Bible are the word of the eternal God.

An experience that brings us into harmony with the Word of God will cost the sacrifice of self. It will require humility of mind and a realization of utter dependence upon God. But those who gain this experience will realize the need of working for others, that they also may believe and rejoice in the truth. Very much depends upon the manner in which the truth is presented. The human heart is a hard field to work. Let the missionary ever keep the Word of God upon his lips. Those who talk the truth will have light upon the Word of God. Contemplating the Word of Christ is beholding Christ by the eye of faith. The Word of God is quick and powerful, and coming in contact with the faculties of men, and human mind becomes strong and vigorous, and able to exercise its powers in learning the lesson of sinking self into Christ.

The Bible contains the living bread for the soul. Shall this Book, with its treasures of wisdom, be opened to those who are unlearned, and especially to the vast numbers of the colored people who are scattered through the United States? Shall we be justified in withholding this precious Word from the ignorant and depraved, when by partaking of it by faith is eternal life? Shall we expend labor most largely for those who know the truth? Shall weeks be occupied in seeking to work up a greater interest among those who have heard the truth of salvation over and over again, and leave those who have never heard it with no effort for their enlightenment? How much more appropriate would it be for those who have been thus privileged, to expend their time, talent, and money in imparting that which they understand to those who do not know God, and have never had the Scriptures opened up before them—in presenting the special message that is to be given to the world in these last days! Gather up the precious fragments of truth and go to work to present them to those who are starving for the Word of life.

Through the study of the Word of God, a great work may be done for the Southern people. The colored people, though emancipated from physical slavery, are still in the slavery of ignorance. They are led to believe that they should do just what their ministers tell them to do. Unless their minds are enlightened so that they may understand the Scripture for themselves, and know that God has spoken to their souls, they will not be benefited by the preaching of the truth; for they are in a condition to be deceived easily by false teachers. In reaching the colored people, it is best to seek to educate them before presenting the pointed truths of the third angel's message. Let missionaries work quietly for both white and colored people in the South. Let them work in a way to help those who most need help, who are surrounded with influences that are misleading. Many of them are under the control of those who will stir up the worst passions of the human heart. The priests and rulers in Christ's day worked most successfully in stirring up the passions of the mob, because they were ignorant, and had placed their trust in man. Thus they were led to denounce and reject Christ and to choose a robber and murderer in His place. The work in the South should be done without noise or parade. Let missionaries who are truly converted, and who feel the burden of the work, seek wisdom from God, and with all the tact they can command, let them go into this field. Medical missionaries can find a field in which to relieve the distress of those who are failing under bodily ailments. They should have means so that they may clothe the naked and feed the hungry. Christian help work will do more than the preaching of sermons. There is a great need that a class of workers should go to this field who will do this kind of work. Let them meet together and relate their experiences, pray together, and hold their services, not in a way to attract attention to themselves, but in quietness, in meekness, and lowliness. But while they pursue this humble course, let them not sink down into cheapness in conversation, cheapness in manners and ways. Let the workers be Christlike, that they may by precept and example exert an elevating influence. Let them furnish themselves with the most appropriate, simple lessons from the life of

Christ to present to the people. Let them not dwell too much upon doctrinal points, or upon features of our faith that will seem strange and new; but let them present the sufferings and the sacrifice of Christ; let them hold up His righteousness and reveal His grace; let them manifest His purity and holiness of character. Workers in the Southern field will need to teach the people line upon line, precept upon precept, here a little and there a little.

As men and women embrace the truth in this field, there will be abundant opportunity for relieving their pressing necessities. Unless this can be done, the work will largely prove a failure. To say, Be ye warmed, and be ye clothed, and be ye fed, and take no steps to bring these things to pass, will have a bad influence upon our work. Object lessons will be of far more value than mere precepts. Deeds of sympathy will be needed as well as words that will touch the heart and leave an uneffaceable impression upon the mind. Small schools should be established in many localities, and teachers who are tender and sympathetic, who can, like the Master, be touched by suffering, should be engaged to educate old and young. Let the Word of God be taught in the simplest manner. Let the pupils be led to study the lessons of Christ; for the study of the Bible will do more to enlarge the mind and strengthen the intellect than will any other study. Nothing will so awaken the dormant energies and give vigor to the faculties as coming in contact with the Word of God.

There is much talent among the colored people. Their minds must be aroused, their intellects quickened into activity, that they may grasp the precious truths of the plan of salvation. Their minds have become dwarfed and enfeebled, because they have been called out and exercised upon commonplace matters, and have been occupied with low, cheap ideas. But as elevating truths are repeated, their minds will expand, and their ability increase to take in and comprehend the subjects with which they become more familiar. A field left uncultivated will soon be filled with unsightly weeds and thistles. The mind left uncultivated will be filled with that which is unsightly, and where seeds of truth are not sown, there will be no fruit of a heavenly order. The colored people have been left in ignorance, and the minds of many have lost the ability to expand. But many are not satisfied. They hunger for something they have not. Were they educated so that they could read the Bible, they would draw comfort from the plan of salvation as it is revealed in Jesus Christ. The influence of truth would work for the enlargement of their minds and the strengthening of their faculties. Thus they would be enabled to grasp other branches of knowledge, and prepared to receive information of a general character. (*The Review and Herald,* December 24, 1895)

Chapter 7

Spirit and Life for the Colored People

The psalmist says, "The entrance of thy words giveth light; it giveth understanding unto the simple." Heavenly intelligences are close by the side of every one who is seeking to open the Word of God to the understanding of the simple, or to those who are really desirous of becoming acquainted with the will of God. Those who open the scripture to others should teach them the Word of life, realizing the solemn, sacred work that they are doing; for they are bringing souls in contact with God and with Jesus Christ, whom He has sent. Any trifling, jesting, or joking over the Word of God is dishonoring to Him, and leaves an influence that is anything but good upon the mind. But if we desire to enlarge a man's mind, let us turn his attention to the Scriptures. In the Bible we behold Him who is the way, the truth, and the life. Through understanding the Word of God, efficiency is obtained for both the practical and the religious life.

Jesus said: "Labor not for the meat which perisheth, but for that meat which endureth unto everlasting life, which the Son of man shall give unto you: for him hath God the Father sealed. Then said they unto him, what shall we do, that we might work the works of God? Jesus answered and said unto them, this is the work of God, that ye believe on him whom he hath sent. They said therefore unto him, what sign shewest thou then, that we may see, and believe thee? What dost thou work? Our fathers did eat manna in the desert; as it is written, He gave them bread from heaven to eat. Then Jesus said unto them, Verily, verily, I say unto you, Moses gave you not that bread from heaven: but my Father giveth you the true bread from heaven. For the bread of God is he which cometh down from heaven, and giveth life unto the world. Then said they unto him, Lord, evermore give us this bread. And Jesus said unto them, I am the bread of life: he that cometh to me shall never hunger; and he that believeth on me shall never thirst.... I am that bread of life. Your fathers did eat manna in the wilderness, and are dead. This is the bread which cometh down from heaven, that a man may eat thereof, and not die. I am the living bread which came down from heaven: if any man eat of this bread, he shall live for ever: and the bread that I will give is my flesh, which I will give for the life of the world.... Verily, verily, I say unto you, except ye eat the flesh of the Son of man, and drink his blood, ye have no life in you. Whoso eateth my flesh, and drinketh my blood, hath eternal life; and I will raise him up at the last day. For my flesh is meat indeed, and my blood is drink indeed. He that eateth my flesh, and drinketh my blood, dwelleth in me, and I in him. As the living Father hath sent me, and I live by the Father: so he that eateth me, even he shall live by me." Jesus explained what He meant by eating His flesh and drinking His blood. He meant that His disciples were to partake of His Word. He said, "It is the Spirit that quickeneth; the flesh profiteth nothing: the words that I speak unto you, they are spirit, and they are life."

The Word of Christ is the bread of life that is furnished for every soul that liveth. To refuse to eat this bread is death. He that neglects to partake of the Word of God shall not see life. Receiving the Word is believing the Word, and this is eating Christ's flesh, drinking His blood. To dwell and abide in Christ is to dwell and abide in His Word; it is to bring heart and character into conformity to His commands. In the parable of the vine and the branches, Jesus shows the vital connection that must exist between Himself and His followers. He says: "I am the true vine, and my Father is the husbandman. Every branch in me that beareth not fruit he taketh away: and every branch that beareth fruit, he purgeth it, that it may bring forth more fruit. Now ye are clean through the word which I have spoken unto you. Abide in me, and I in you. As the branch cannot bear fruit of itself, except it abide in the vine; no more can ye, except ye abide in me. I am the vine, ye are the branches: He that abideth in me, and I in him, the same bringeth forth much fruit: for without me ye can do nothing."

The branches represent the believers in Jesus Christ. Those who truly believe, will do the same works that He did. They are united to Christ by the faith that works by love and purifies the soul. As the branch is nourished by the sap which flows from the parent stock, so the believer in Christ is sustained by the life of Christ. The branches represent the very youngest of the followers of Christ, as the branch includes all the tiny tendrils that belong to it. Jesus is our center. He is the parent stock that bears the branches. In Him our eternal life is centered. The words that He has spoken unto us are spirit and life, and those who feed upon his Word, and are doers of his Word, represent Him in character. His patience, meekness, humility, and love pervade their hearts. Jesus said, "Herein is my Father glorified, that ye bear much fruit; so shall ye be my disciples." If we are indeed grafted into the true vine, we shall bear fruit similar to that of the parent stock.

Those who love Christ will do the works of Christ. They will go forth to seek and to save that which was lost. They will not shun those who are despised, and turn aside from the colored race. They will teach them how to read and how to perform manual labor, educating them to till the soil and to follow trades of various kinds. They will put forth painstaking efforts to develop the capabilities of the people. The cotton field will not be the only resource for a livelihood to the colored people. There will be awakened in them the thought that they are of value with God, and that they are esteemed as His property. The work pointed out is a most needful missionary enterprise. It is the best restitution that can be made to those who have been robbed of their time and deprived of their education. The fact that this is the case leaves a heavy debt upon the American nation. As a nation, we have been made the depositary of sacred truth, and we are to impart the precious knowledge of the Word of God to others. Every earthly blessing has come to us because of the infinite price that has been paid in our behalf. If it has cost so great a price to redeem man, so that he should not perish, but have everlasting life, how we should rejoice that we are privileged to become co-workers with Christ in saving those for whom He has given His precious life! The Lord Jesus loves those for whom He has made the greatest sacrifice. He gave His own most precious life to bring life and immortality to light to all those who should believe. "This is life eternal, that they might know thee the only true God, and Jesus Christ, whom thou hast sent." Those who receive Christ are in copartnership with Him, and will not mistake their lifework. They will heed the words spoken by Christ. They will be guided by the Holy Spirit, and become more and more intelligent in regard to the requirements of God, and will reveal the love and grace that were revealed in the life of Christ toward those with whom He came in contact. (*The Review and Herald,* January 14, 1896)

Chapter 8

"Am I My Brother's Keeper?"

The law of God contained in the Ten Commandments reveals to man his duty to love God supremely and his neighbor as himself. The American nation owes a debt of love to the colored race, and God has ordained that they should make restitution for the wrong they have done them in the past. Those who have taken no active part in enforcing slavery upon the colored people are not relieved from the responsibility of making special efforts to remove, as far as possible, the sure result of their enslavement.

When the duty of bringing the gospel to the colored race is presented, many make the plea that association with the colored people will contaminate society. But this very plea is evidence that means should be instituted to remove from this race the degradation that has been brought upon them. As a people we should no longer say by our attitude, "Am I my brother's keeper?" We should arouse ourselves to do justly, to love mercy. We should make manifest by our actions that we have the faith for which the saints are to contend. We should go forth to seek the oppressed, to lift up the fallen, and to bring help to those who need our assistance. We should remember that many among the colored people who have been entrusted with God-given ability, who had intellectual capabilities far superior to those of the masters who claimed them as their property, were forced to endure every indignity, and their souls groaned under the most cruel and unjust oppression. They were ambitious to obtain their freedom, and sought in every possible way to obtain it. At times their deferred hope caused them to flash out with indignation, and they were forced to suffer such fearful punishments that their courage was broken, and to all outward appearances their spirits were subdued. But others planned for years, and finally were successful in gaining their freedom. Many of these have filled positions of trust, and have demonstrated the fact that the colored race is capable of cultivation and improvement. As a people claiming to be proclaiming the last message of mercy to the world, we cannot consistently neglect the Southern field, for it is a portion of God's moral vineyard. It is not our place to study consequences, but we are to go to the field and labor for the colored people as earnestly as for the white people, and leave results with God. It is our part to work with all our God-given capabilities to redeem the time that we have wasted in planning how to avoid unhappy results in working the Southern fields.

We are God's messengers, and He has sent us forth to work for both the white and the black race without partiality and without hypocrisy. We are to set forth the truth in warnings and entreaties. We are to point out the path of light in plain and simple language, easy to be understood by both white and black. We have no time to build up walls of distinction between the white and the black race. The white people who embrace the truth in the Southern field, if converted to God, will discern the fact that the plan of redemption embraces every soul that God has created. The walls of sectarianism and caste and race will fall down when the true missionary spirit enters the hearts of men. Prejudice is melted away by the love of God. All will realize that they are to become laborers together with God. Both the Ethiopian and the white race are God's purchased possession, and our work is to improve every talent that has been lent to us of God, to save the souls of both white and black. If men and women of either race refuse the truth of God, they must answer to God for their rejection of Jesus Christ, who died for their salvation. With all our might we must do our work now.

God's object in bringing us to Himself is to conform us to the image of Christ Jesus. All who believe in Christ will understand the personal relation that exists between them and their brethren. They are to be as branches grafted into the same parent stock, to draw sustenance from the root. Believers, whether white or black, are branches of the True Vine. There is to be no special heaven for the white man and another heaven for the black man. We are all to be saved through the same grace, all to enter the same heaven at last. Then why not act like rational beings, and overcome our unlikeness to Christ? The same God that blesses us as His sons and daughters blesses the colored race. Those who have the faith that works by love and purifies the soul will look with compassion and love upon the colored people. Many of those who have had every advantage, who have regarded themselves as superior to the colored people because their skin was white, will find that many of the colored race will go into heaven before them.

Let every one who values the precious sacrifice made by Jesus Christ, lift up his voice in prayer to God, and exclaim: "Behold, O Lord, this poor, oppressed people that have been despised and maltreated by the white nation. Breathe into their souls the breath of spiritual life. If no effort is made on their behalf, they will perish in their sins, and their blood will be found upon our garments. Father of mercies, pity thine offspring. Breathe upon these beaten, bruised, ignorant souls, that they may live. Give thy Holy Spirit to those who shall go forth as messengers to this people. Take not thy Holy Spirit from us in our councils, and enable us to make plans and devise means for the spread of the truth among them."

We need to awaken, and to understand the truth as it is in Jesus. We need to consult the Word of God, in order that we shall not seek to evade disagreeable work. When we realize that we are workers together with God, the promises will not be spoken with half indifference, but will burn in our hearts, and kindle on our lips. We shall present them to the throne of God with earnestness, and the Lord will pour out His Spirit upon the devoted, consecrated worker. Those who plead with

God, as did Moses, will receive the same assurances that Moses received. When Moses pleaded: "I pray thee, if I have found grace in thy sight, shew me now thy way, that I may know thee, that I may find grace in thy sight: and consider that this nation is thy people. And He said, My presence shall go with thee, and I will give thee rest." Again the Lord said to Moses, "Certainly I will be with thee." The same assurances given to Moses will be given to those who go forth to be colaborers with Jesus Christ in the Southern field. We are not to wait for great men to undertake the work. We are to encourage those who have a burden to go to this field, who are willing to undertake the work. Let those in responsible positions give their sympathy to such workers, and furnish them with facilities whereby they may do the work required. Let not men in our institutions feel that it is their prerogative to tie the hands of workers at every step. Let those who have a mind to work, do with their might whatsoever their hands find to do. Let those who take no part in the trying experience of teaching the colored people, unite their petitions with those of the workers, and plead that the Holy Spirit may move upon the hearts of the workers and aid them in doing successful work for the Master. The Lord God of Sabaoth will hear earnest prayer. He will lead those who feel their dependence upon Him, and will so guide the workers that many souls shall come to a knowledge of the truth.

Truth as it is in Jesus exercises a transforming influence upon the minds of its receivers. Let no one forget that God is always a majority, and that with Him success is bound to crown all missionary effort. Those who have a living connection with God know that divinity works through humanity. Every soul that cooperates with God will do justly, love mercy, and walk humbly with God. The Lord is a God of mercy, and cares even for the dumb beasts He has created. When He healed on the Sabbath day, and was accused of breaking the law of God, He said to his accusers: "Doth not each one of you on the sabbath loose his ox or his ass from the stall, and lead him away to watering? And ought not this woman, being a daughter of Abraham, whom Satan hath bound, lo, these eighteen years, be loosed from this bond on the sabbath day? And when he had said these things, all his adversaries were ashamed: and all the people rejoiced for all the glorious things that were done by him." The Lord looks upon the creatures He has made with compassion, no matter to what race they may belong. God "Hath made of one blood all nations of men for to dwell on all the face of the earth, and hath determined the times before appointed, and the bounds of their habitation; that they should seek the Lord, if haply they might feel after him, and find him, though he be not far from every one of us: for in him we live, and move, and have our being; as certain also of your own poets have said, for we are also his offspring." Speaking to His disciples the Savior said, "All ye are brethren." God is our common Father, and each one of us is our brother's keeper. (*The Review and Herald*, January 21, 1896)

Chapter 9

Lift Up Your Eyes and Look on the Field

Those who work in the Southern field will need to have a sanctified judgment, in order to discriminate in applying help where it will do the greatest amount of good. They should help those who will be a help to others, as well as those who may not be able to carry on very decided missionary operations. I know that it will be impossible for workers to remain in this field in a bare-handed condition and do the work that is required to be done in the Southern States. It will be necessary that a fund shall be created so that the workers may have means with which to help those who are in poverty and distress, and this practical ministry will open their hearts to respond to the truth.

It will be necessary for the worker in the Southern field not only to have an appreciation of the physical wants of the colored people, but his heart must also be aglow with the love of God. He must present the love of God with faith and assurance, and not follow any bleak, cold, methodical style. The Southern field is a field where the religious instruction will have to be repeated again and again. The language must be most simple in style, for many of the colored people are only children in understanding; but though this field has been long neglected, the words of Christ are applicable to it. Our Lord said to His disciples, "Say not ye, there are yet four months, and then cometh harvest? Behold, I say unto you, lift up your eyes, and look on the fields; for they are white already to harvest. And he that reapeth receiveth wages, and gathereth fruit unto life eternal: that both he that soweth and he that reapeth may rejoice together."

When the Lord spoke these words to the disciples, they did not see anything that denoted that they were in an encouraging field. The seed of truth had been sown, and the harvest was about to follow. While they had been away purchasing food, Christ had preached a sermon to the woman at the well, and had sown the seed, and the harvest was to come forth speedily. She had gone back into the city of Samaria and had spread abroad the words of Christ. She gave the invitation to those she met, saying with assurance, "Come, see a man, which told me all things that ever I did: is not this the Christ?" Jesus knew that at the report of the woman many, out of curiosity, would come to see and to hear Him, and that many would believe on Him, and drink of the water of life that He should give them. "And many of the Samaritans of that city believed on him for the saying of the woman, which testified, He told me all that ever I did. So when the Samaritans were come unto him, they besought him that he would tarry with them: and he abode there two days. And many more believed because of his own word; and said unto the woman, now we believe, not because of thy saying: for we have heard him ourselves, and know that this is indeed the Christ, the Savior of the world." Thus the harvest came speedily after the sowing, for the Holy Spirit had impressed the truth upon the hearts of the Samaritans.

The words that Jesus spoke to His disciples, saying that the fields were white for the harvest, are addressed to every genuine Christian. We also are to look upon the fields, and see the necessities of men. The disciples were encouraged as they saw the readiness of the Samaritans to receive the truth. They had regarded this field as a very hard field, and yet they saw men acknowledging the words of the Master, and believing on Him for themselves. This lesson is for our encouragement as well, and while there are many who will not yield to the convicting power of God's Spirit, there are also many who are hungering for the words of light and salvation. Many will receive the truth, and testify as did the Samaritans that Christ is the Savior of the world. In their turn they will become sowers of the seed of truth. We are to lift up our eyes and look upon the fields that are white already for the harvest. For years we have passed by the Southern field, and have looked upon the colored race, feebly deploring their condition; but our eyes have been fastened upon more promising fields. But now God's people should lift up their eyes and look upon this destitute field that has not been worked. The missionary spirit must prevail if we form characters after the pattern, Christ Jesus. We are to love our neighbors as ourselves, and the colored people, in the sight of God, are our neighbors. It is not enough for us merely to look on and deplore the discouraging appearance of the field, and then pass by on the other side and do nothing. Unitedly and interestedly we must take hold of the work. We are not only to look upon the fields, but we are to reap, and gather fruit unto life eternal.

God calls us to consider and to help those who are in most need of help. As workers together with God, we are not simply to deplore the destitute condition of the Southern people, but we are to seek to alleviate their condition. Here is a field in America that is nigh at hand. One is to sow the seed, another to reap the harvest, another to bind it up. There is a variety of work, which must be done now while the angels continue to hold the four winds. Many who desire to do missionary work may labor in this field. There is no time to be lost. As men, women, and children among the colored people receive the truth, they should be instructed by those who are imbued with the Spirit of God, and educated and directed in such a way that they may help others.

The Southern field is right in the shadow of your own doors. It is as land that has had a touch of the plow here and there, and then has been left by the plowman, who has been attracted to some easier or more promising field; but those who work the Southern field must make up their minds to practice self-denial. Those who would aid in this work must also practice self-denial, in order that facilities may be provided whereby the field may be worked. God calls for missionaries, and asks us to take up our neglected duties. Let farmers, financiers, builders, and those who are skilled in various arts and crafts go to this field to improve lands and to build humble cottages for themselves and their neighbors. Christ says to you, lift up your eyes, and look upon this Southern field; for it needs the sowers of seed and the reapers of grain. The grace of Christ is unlimited; it is God's free gift. Why should not this neglected people have the benefit of divine hope and courage and faith? All those who will accept Christ will have sunlight in the heart, and the wholehearted, unselfish worker will receive a reward. Those who are laborers together with God will enter into the joy of their Lord. What is this joy? It is the joy that is felt in the presence of the angels over one sinner that repenteth more than over ninety and nine just persons who need no repentance.

Those who labor in the Southern field will meet with deplorable ignorance. The colored people are suffering the results of the bondage in which they were held. When they were slaves they were taught to do the will of those who called them their property. They were kept in ignorance, and today there are thousands among them that cannot read. Many who profess to be teachers among them are corrupt in character, and they interpret the Scriptures in such a way as to fulfil their own purposes and degrade those who are in their power. The colored people are taught that they must not think or judge for themselves, but that their ministers must be permitted to judge for them. Because of this, the divine plan of salvation has been covered up with a mass of human rubbish and falsehood. The Scripture has been perverted, and the people have been perverted, and the people have been so instructed as to be easily seduced by evil spirits. Mind as well as body has been long abused. The whole system of slavery was originated by Satan, who delights in tyrannizing over human beings. Though he has been successful in degrading and corrupting the black race, many are possessed of decided ability, and if they were blessed with opportunities, they would show more intelligence than do many of their more favored brethren among the white people. Thousands may now be uplifted, and may become agents by which to help those of their own race. There are many who feel the necessity of becoming elevated, and when faithful teachers open the Scriptures, presenting the truth in its native purity to the colored people, the darkness will be dispelled under the bright beams of the Sun of righteousness. Directed in their search for truth by those who have had advantages enabling them to know the truth, they will become intelligent in the Scriptures.

When laws are enacted that bind the consciences of those whom God has made free, and men are cast into prison for exercising their religious liberty, many poor, timid, ignorant souls will be hindered from doing the will of God; but many will learn aright from Jesus Christ, and will maintain their God-given freedom at any cost. The colored people have been slow to learn what is their right in religious liberty, because of the attitude that men have assumed toward them. In many minds there is great confusion in regard to what is individual right. Men have exercised compelling power over the mind and judgment of the colored race. Satan is the originator of all oppression, and history shows a record of the terrible results of oppressive tortures that have been endured by men who are God's property, both by creation and by redemption. Through human agencies, Satan has manifested his own attributes and passions; but every act of injustice, every fraudulent purpose, every pang of anguish, is written down in the books of heaven as done against Christ Jesus, who has purchased man at an infinite price. The manner in which men treat their fellow men is registered as done unto Christ; but those who have been faithful winners of souls will receive commendation, and will join in the song of those who rejoice, and shout the harvest home. How great will be the joy when the redeemed of the Lord will all meet together in the mansions prepared for them! What rejoicing will come to those who have been impartial, unselfish laborers together with God in winning souls to Christ! What satisfaction will fill the breast of every reaper when he hears the musical voice of Jesus saying, "Well done, thou good and faithful servant; ... Enter thou into the joy of thy Lord!"

Those who win souls to Christ glorify their Redeemer. He has not died in vain for them, for they are in harmony with Christ. They look upon those who have turned to God through their efforts, with glad rejoicing; for they also see of the travail of their souls, and are satisfied. They see that the anxious hours they have spent, the perplexing circumstances they have had to meet, the sorrows they have had to endure, have worked for them a far more exceeding and eternal weight of glory. As they look upon the souls they have won to Christ, and know that they are eternally saved, are monuments of God's mercy and of a Redeemer's love, they touch the golden harp and fill the arches of heaven with praise and thanksgiving. They sing, "Thou wast slain, and hast redeemed us to God by thy blood out of every kindred, and tongue, and people, and nation; and hast made us unto our God Kings and priests: and we shall reign on the earth.... Worthy is the Lamb that was slain to receive power, and riches, and wisdom, and strength, and honor, and glory, and blessing."

"They that be wise shall shine as the brightness of the firmament; and they that turn many to righteousness as the stars for ever and ever." How great is the reward that will come to those who devote their God-given abilities to doing the works of Christ. Those who are partakers of His sufferings in this world will be partakers of His glory in the world hereafter, and will sit down with Christ upon His throne. (*The Review and Herald,* January 28, 1896)

Chapter 10

Volunteers Wanted for the Southern Field

Instruction is to be given to our colored neighbors concerning the physical, mental, and moral nature. We must give them line upon line, precept upon precept, here a little, and there a little. The youth will catch the lessons that are given, and retain them much more readily than those who are aged. How important it is that this large class of human beings, who are now in ignorance, should be taught to read for themselves, that they may know what saith the Lord unto them! How anxious every Christian family should be to have a part in helping on the education of the colored race! Many of them are poor, neglected, homeless creatures. We should teach them how to build cheap houses, how to erect school buildings in cities and villages, and how to carry on their education.

God holds us accountable for our long neglect of doing our duty to our neighbors. He sees precious jewels that will shine out from among the colored race. Let the work be taken up determinedly, and let both the young and those of mature age be educated in essential branches. Take hold of this nation that has been in bondage, as the Lord Jesus Christ took hold of the Hebrew nation after they came forth from Egypt. God will put His Holy Spirit upon those who put heart and soul into the work, realizing the truth of the words of inspiration: "We are laborers together with God: ye are God's husbandry, ye are God's building." The Lord has long been waiting for human instrumentalities through whom He could work. How much longer shall heavenly agencies be obliged to wait for human agents who will respond to the words of Christ, "Go work to day in my vineyard"? When the hearts of God's professed people are animated by the principle of the living faith that works by love and purifies the soul, there will be a response to these appeals. Christ linked Himself in brotherhood to all nationalities. He made no distinction between the white race and the black race in His plan of salvation. He bought the meanest of humanity with an infinite price, and He notes when we leave the naked unclad, the poor unfed, the destitute unrelieved, the despised forsaken.

Those who labor in the Southern field will have many prejudices to overcome, many difficulties to encounter. At the present time there is great want among many of the colored people. Self-denial must be practiced by us. We must strip ourselves of all extravagance; we must deny ourselves luxuries and the undue gratification of appetite. Let those who have not laid aside unnecessary articles of diet, do so. Let them refrain from adornment and costly furnishings. Let us set ourselves to do a work for the Southern people. Let us not be content with simply looking on, with simply making resolutions that are never acted upon; but let us do something heartily unto the Lord, to alleviate the distress of our colored brethren. The burden of poverty is sufficiently weighty to arouse our heartfelt sympathy. We are not simply to say, "Be ye warmed and filled," But we are actually to relieve the needs of the poor. Filthiness is prevalent among the colored people, and it is a breeder of disease. Discouragement is deep and widespread, and shall we refuse to stretch forth our hands to help in this time of peril?

But it is of no use to send missionaries to work in the Southern field unless they are furnished with means from your abundance to help the distressed and those who are in poverty that cannot be described. We may do the work that Christ would do if He were upon earth. We may relieve those whose lives have been one long scene of sorrow. Who will go on in indifference and pay no attention to the woes of those who are in hunger, in nakedness, in ignorance and degradation? Who will rouse up and go without the camp and bear reproach for Christ's sake? Who will put on Christ and seek to rescue their colored brethren from ignominy, crime, and degradation? Who will seek to restore them to the ranks of common humanity? We must not consider them irreclaimable and utterly degenerate. With the spirit of Christ, who did not fail or become discouraged, we may do a work that will cause the heavenly hosts to fill the courts of God with songs of rejoicing. There are many who are looked upon as stoical; who are thought to be unfit to be taught the gospel of Jesus Christ; and yet through the ministration of the Holy Spirit they may be changed by the miracle of divine grace. The stupidity that makes their cases look so hopeless will pass away, for it is the result of great ignorance. The influence of grace will prevail on the human subject, and the dull and clouded mind will awake and break its fetters. Through divine power the slave to sin may be set free. The sunshine of Christ's righteousness may beam into the chambers of mind and heart. Spiritual life will be seen, and the brutishness will disappear. Inclination to vice will disappear, and ignorance will be overcome. The heart will be purified by the faith that works by love.

There are thousands who are capable of instruction, cultivation, and elevation. With proper, persevering labor, many who have been considered hopeless cases will become educators of their race. The colored people deserve much more from the hands of the white people than they have received. The colored people may be compared to a mine that is to be worked, in which is valuable ore of most precious material. Christ has given these people souls capable of winning and enjoying immortal life in the kingdom of God. One tenth of the advantages that their more favored brethren have received and failed to improve, would cause them to become mediums of light through which the brightness of the righteousness of Christ might shine forth. Who will enlist in this work, and willingly teach the ignorant what saith the Word of God? Who will engage in the work of quickening the mental faculties into sensibility, of uplifting those who are downtrodden? Can we not show that we are willing to try to repair as far as possible the injury that has been done to them in the past? Shall not missionaries be multiplied? Shall we hear of volunteers, who are willing to go into the field to bring souls out of darkness and ignorance into the marvelous light in which we rejoiced, that they also may see the glory of God in the face of Jesus Christ? "And this is life eternal, that they might know thee the only true God, and Jesus Christ, whom thou hast sent." (*The Review and Herald,* February 4, 1896)

Chapter 11

Our Duty to the Colored People

There has been much perplexity as to how our laborers in the South shall deal with the "color line." It has been a question to some how far to concede to the prevailing prejudice against the colored people. The Lord has given us light concerning all such matters. There are principles laid down in His Word that should guide us in dealing with these perplexing questions. The Lord Jesus came to our world to save men and women of all nationalities. He died just as much for the colored people as for the white race. Jesus came to shed light over the whole world. At the beginning of His ministry He declared His mission: "The Spirit of the Lord is upon me, because he hath anointed me to preach the gospel to the poor; he hath sent me to heal the brokenhearted, to preach deliverance to the captives, and recovering of sight to the blind, to set at liberty them that are bruised, to preach the acceptable year of the Lord."

The Redeemer of the world was of humble parentage. He, the Majesty of heaven, the King of glory, humbled Himself to accept humanity, and then He chose a life of poverty and toil. "For your sakes he became poor, that ye through his poverty might be rich." When one came saying, "I will follow thee whithersoever thou goest," Jesus answered him, "The foxes have holes, and the birds of the air have nests; but the Son of man hath not where to lay his head." He, the Majesty of heaven, depended upon the generosity of His followers.

Jesus did not seek the admiration or applause of the world. He commanded no army, He ruled no earthly kingdom. He passed by the wealthy and honored of the world. He did not associate with the leaders of the nation. He dwelt among the lowly of the earth. To all appearances he was merely a humble man, with few friends. Thus He sought to correct the world's false standard of judging the value of men. He showed that they are not to be estimated by their outward appearance. Their moral worth is not determined by their worldly possessions, their real estate or bank stock. It is the humble, contrite heart that God values. With Him there is no respect of persons. The attributes that He prizes most are purity and love, and these are possessed only by the Christian.

Jesus did not choose His disciples from the learned lawyers, the rulers, the scribes, and Pharisees. He passed them by because they felt whole, as many feel in this age, and prided themselves on their learning and position. They were fixed in their traditions and superstitions, teaching for doctrines the commandments of men. He who could read all hearts chose poor fishermen who were willing to be taught. He gave them no promise of large salary or worldly honor, but told them they should be partakers with Him in His sufferings. Jesus while in this world ate with publicans and sinners, and mingled with the common people, not to become low and earthly with them, but in order by precept and example to present to them right principles, to lift them up from their low habits and manners. In all this He set us an example, that we should follow in His steps.

Those who have a religious experience that opens their hearts to Jesus, will not cherish pride, but will feel that they are under obligation to God to be missionaries as was Jesus. They will seek to save that which was lost. They will not, in Pharisaical pride and haughtiness, withdraw themselves from any class of humanity, but will feel with the apostle Paul, "I am debtor both to the Greek, and to the barbarians; both to the wise, and to the unwise."

After my severe illness one year ago, many things which the Lord had presented to me seemed lost to my mind, but they have since been repeated. I know that which I now speak will bring me into conflict. This I do not covet, for the conflict has seemed to be continuous of late years; but I do not mean to live a coward or die a coward, leaving my work undone. I must follow in my Master's footsteps. It has become fashionable to look down upon the poor, and upon the colored race in particular. But Jesus, the Master, was poor, and He sympathizes with the poor, the discarded, the oppressed, and declares that every insult shown to them is as if shown to Himself. I am more and more surprised as I see those who claim to be children of God possessing so little of the sympathy, tenderness, and love which actuated Christ. Would that every church, North and South, were imbued with the spirit of our Lord's teaching.

While at St. Louis a year ago, as I knelt in prayer, these words were presented to me as if written with a pen of fire: "All ye are brethren." The Spirit of God rested upon me in a wonderful manner, and matters were opened to me in regard to the church at St. Louis and in other places. The spirit and words of some in regard to members of the church were an offense to God. They were closing the door of their hearts to Jesus. Among those in St. Louis who believe the truth there are colored people who are true and faithful, precious in the sight of the God of heaven, and they should have just as much respect as any of God's children. Those who have spoken harshly to them or have despised them have despised the purchase of the blood of Christ, and they need the transforming grace of Christ in their own hearts, that they may have the pitying tenderness of Jesus toward those who love God with all the fervor of which they themselves are capable. The color of the skin does not determine character in the heavenly courts.

"If ye call on the Father, who without respect of persons judgeth according to every man's work, pass the time of your sojourning here in fear: forasmuch as ye know that ye were not redeemed with corruptible things, as silver and gold, from your vain conversation received by tradition from your fathers; but with the precious blood of Christ, as of a lamb without blemish and without spot.... Seeing ye have purified your souls in obeying the truth through the Spirit unto unfeigned love of the brethren, see that ye love one another with a pure heart fervently." "Ye have put off the old man with his deeds; and have put on the new man, which is renewed in knowledge after the image of him that created him: wherefore there is neither Greek nor Jew, circumcision nor uncircumcision, Barbarian, Scythian, bond nor free: but Christ is all, and in all. Put on therefore, as the elect of God, holy and beloved, bowels of mercies, kindness, humbleness of mind, meekness, longsuffering."

"Who," says Paul, "maketh thee to differ?" The God of the white man is the God of the black man, and the Lord declares that His love for the least of His children exceeds that of a mother for her beloved child. Look at that mother: the sick child, the one afflicted, the one born a cripple, or with some other physical infirmity—how the mother labors to give him every advantage! The best food, the softest pillow, and the tenderest nursing are for him. The love bestowed upon him is strong and deep—a love such as is not given to beauty, talent, or any other natural gift. As soon as a mother sees reason for others to regard her child with aversion or contempt, does she not increase her tenderness as if to shield him from the world's rude touch? "Can a mother forget her sucking child . . .? yea, they may forget, yet I will not forget thee." O what impartial love the Lord Jesus gives to those who love Him! The Lord's eye is upon all His creatures; He loves them all, and makes no difference between white and black, except that He has a special, tender pity for those who are called to bear a greater burden than others. Those who love God and believe on Christ as their Redeemer, while they must meet the trials and the difficulties that lie in their path, should yet with a cheerful spirit accept their life as it is, considering that God above regards these things, and for all that the world neglects to bestow, He will Himself make up to them in the best of favors.

The parable of Dives, the rich man, and Lazarus, the poor beggar who feared God, is presented before the world as a lesson to all, both rich and poor, as long as time shall last. Dives is represented as lifting up his eyes in hell, being in torments, and seeing Abraham afar off, and Lazarus in his bosom,—"he cried and said, Father Abraham, have mercy on me, and send Lazarus, that he may dip the tip of his finger in water, and cool my tongue; for I am tormented in this flame. But Abraham said, Son, remember that thou in thy lifetime receivedst thy good things, and likewise Lazarus evil things; but now he is comforted, and thou art tormented."

When the sinner is converted he receives the Holy Spirit, that makes him a child of God, and fits him for the society of the redeemed and the angelic host. He is made a joint heir with Christ. Whoever of the human family give themselves to Christ, whoever hear the truth and obey it, become children of one family. The ignorant and the wise, the rich and the poor, the heathen and the slave, white or black—Jesus paid the purchase money for their souls. If they believe on Him, His cleansing blood is applied to them. The black man's name is written in the book of life beside the white man's. All are one in Christ. Birth, station, nationality, or color cannot elevate or degrade men. The character makes the man. If a red man, a Chinaman, or an African gives his heart to God, in obedience and faith, Jesus loves him none the less for his color. He calls him his well-beloved brother. The day is coming when the kings and the lordly men of the earth would be glad to exchange places with the humblest African who has laid hold on the hope of the gospel. To all who are overcomers through the blood of the Lamb, the invitation will be given, "Come, ye blessed of my Father, inherit the kingdom prepared for you from the foundation of the world." Arranged on the right and left of the throne of God are the long columns of the heavenly host, who touch the golden harps, and the songs of welcome and of praise to God and the Lamb ring through the heavenly courts. "He that hath an ear, let him hear what the Spirit saith unto the churches; To him that overcometh will I give to eat of the tree of life, which is in the midst of the paradise of God."

Among what are called the higher classes, there is a demand for a form of Christianity suited to their fine tastes; but this class will not grow up to the full stature of men and women in Christ until they know God and Jesus Christ whom He has sent. The heavenly intelligences rejoice to do the will of God in preaching the gospel to the poor. In the announcement which the Savior made in the synagogue at Nazareth, He put a stern rebuke upon those who attach so much importance to color or caste, and refuse to be satisfied with such a type of Christianity as Christ accepts. The same price was paid for the salvation of the colored man as for that of the white man, and the slights put upon the colored people by many who claim to be redeemed by the blood of the Lamb, and who therefore acknowledge themselves debtors to Christ, misrepresent Jesus, and reveal that selfishness, tradition, and prejudice pollute the soul. They are not sanctified through the truth. Those who slight a brother because of his color are slighting Christ.

I call upon every church in our land to look well to your own souls. "Examine yourselves, whether ye be in the faith; prove your own selves. Know ye not your own selves, how that Jesus Christ is in you, except ye be reprobates?" God makes no distinction between the North and the South. Whatever may be your prejudices, your wonderful prudence, do not lose sight of this fact, that unless you put on Christ, and His Spirit dwells in you, you are slaves of sin and of Satan. Many who claim to be children of God are children of the wicked one, and have all his passions, his prejudices, his evil spirit, his unlovely traits of character. But the soul that is indeed transformed will not despise any one whom Christ has purchased with His own blood.

Men may have both hereditary and cultivated prejudices, but when the love of Jesus fills the heart, and they become one with Christ, they will have the same spirit that He had. If a colored brother sits by their side, they will not be offended or despise him. They are journeying to the same heaven, and will be seated at the same table to eat bread in the kingdom of God. If Jesus is abiding in our hearts we cannot despise the colored man who has the same Savior abiding in his heart. When these unchristian prejudices are broken down, more earnest effort will be put forth to do missionary work among the colored race.

When the Hebrew people were suffering cruel oppression under the hand of their taskmasters, the Lord looked upon them, and He called Israel His son. He bade Moses go to Pharaoh with the message, "Israel is my son, even my firstborn. And I say unto thee, Let my son go, that he may serve me." The Lord did not wait until His people went forth and stood in triumph on the shores of the Red Sea before He called Israel His son, but while they were under oppression, degraded, downtrodden, suffering all that the power and the invention of the Egyptians could impose to make their lives bitter and to destroy them, then God undertakes their cause and declares to Pharaoh, "Israel is my son, even my firstborn."

What thoughts and feelings did the message arouse in Pharaoh? "This people, my slaves, those whom the lowest of my people despise, the God of such a people I care not for, neither will I let Israel go." But the word of the Lord will not return unto Him void; it will accomplish the thing whereunto it is sent. The Lord speaks in no uncertain manner. He says, "Let my son go, that he may serve me: and if thou refuse to let him go, behold, I will slay thy son, even thy firstborn."

God cares no less for the souls of the African race that might be won to serve Him than He cared for Israel. He requires far more of His people than they have given Him in missionary work among the people of the South of all classes, and especially among the colored race. Are we not under even greater obligation to labor for the colored people than for those who have been more highly favored? Who is it that held these people in servitude? Who kept them in ignorance, and pursued a course to debase and brutalize them, forcing them to disregard the law of marriage, breaking up the family relation, tearing wife from husband, and husband from wife? If the race is degraded, if they are repulsive in habits and manners, who made them so? Is there not much due to them from the white people? After so great a wrong has been done them, should not an earnest effort be made to lift them up? The truth must be carried to them. They have souls to save as well as we.

At the General Conference of 1889, resolutions were presented in regard to the color line. Such action is not called for. Let not men take the place of God, but stand aside in awe, and let God work upon human hearts, both white and black, in His own way. He will adjust all these perplexing questions. We need not prescribe a definite plan of working. Leave an opportunity for God to do something. We should be careful not to strengthen prejudices that ought to have died just as soon as Christ redeemed the soul from the bondage of sin.

Sin rests upon us as a church because we have not made greater effort for the salvation of souls among the colored people. It will always be a difficult matter to deal with the prejudices of the white people in the South and do missionary work for the colored race. But the way this matter has been treated by some is an offense to God. We need not expect that all will be accomplished in the South that God would do until in our missionary efforts we place this question on the ground of principle, and let those who accept the truth be educated to be Bible Christians, working according to Christ's order. You have no license from God to exclude the colored people from your places of worship. Treat them as Christ's property, which they are, just as much as yourselves. They should hold membership in the church with the white brethren. Every effort should be made to wipe out the terrible wrong which has been done them. At the same time we must not carry things to extremes and run into fanaticism on this question. Some would think it right to throw down every partition wall and intermarry with the colored people, but this is not the right thing to teach or to practice.

Let us do what we can to send to this class laborers who will work in Christ's name, who will not fail nor be discouraged. We should educate colored men to be missionaries among their own people. We should recognize talent where it exists among the people, and those who have ability should be placed where they may receive an education.

There are able colored ministers who have embraced the truth. Some of these feel unwilling to devote themselves to work for their own race; they wish to preach to the white people. These men are making a great mistake. They should seek most earnestly to save their own race, and they will not by any means be excluded from the gatherings of the white people.

White men and white women should be qualifying themselves to work among the colored people. There is a large work to be done in educating this ignorant and downtrodden class. We must do more unselfish missionary work than we have done in the Southern States, not picking out merely the most favorable fields. God has children among the colored people all over the land. They need to be enlightened. There are unpromising ones, it is true, but you will find similar degradation among the white people; but even among the lower classes there are souls who will embrace the truth. Some will not be steadfast. Feelings and habits that have been confirmed by lifelong practices will be hard to correct; it will not be easy to implant ideas of purity and holiness, refinement and elevation. But God regards the capacity of every man, He marks the surroundings, and sees how these have formed the character, and He pities these souls.

Is it not time for us to live so fully in the light of God's countenance that we who receive so many favors and blessings from Him may know how to treat those less favored, not working from the world's standpoint, but from the Bible standpoint? Is it not right in this line that Christian effort is most needed? Is it not here that our influence should be brought to bear against the customs and practices of the world? Should it not be the work of the white people to elevate the standard of character among the colored race, to teach them how Christians should live, by exemplifying the Spirit of Christ, showing that we are one brotherhood?

Those who have been favored with opportunities of education and culture, who have had every advantage of religious influence, will be expected of God to possess pure and holy characters in accordance with the gifts bestowed. But have they rightly improved their advantages? We know they have not. Let these privileged ones make the most of their blessings, and realize that they are thus placed under greater obligation to labor for the good of others.

God will accept many more workers from the humble walks of life if they will fully consecrate themselves to His service. Men and women should be coming up to carry the truth into all the highways and byways of life. Not all can go through a long course of education, but if they are consecrated to God and learn of Him, many can without this do much to bless others. Thousands would be accepted if they would give themselves to God. Not all who labor in this line should depend upon the conferences for support. Let those who can do so give their time and what ability they have, let them be messengers of God's grace, their hearts throbbing in unison with Christ's great heart of love, their ears open to hear the Macedonian cry.

The whole church needs to be imbued with the missionary spirit, then there will be many to work unselfishly in various ways as they can, without being salaried. There is altogether too much dependence on machinery, on mechanical working. Machinery is good in its place, but do not allow it to become too complicated. I tell you that in many cases it has retarded the work, and kept out laborers who in their line could have accomplished far more than has been done by the minister who depends on sermonizing more than on ministry. Young men need to catch the missionary spirit, to be thoroughly imbued with the spirit of the message.

"Put ye on the Lord Jesus Christ, and make no provision for the flesh to fulfil the lusts thereof." Work in any capacity, work where God leads you, in the line best suited to your talents and best adapted to reach classes that have hitherto been sadly neglected. This kind of labor will develop intellectual and moral power and adaptability to the work.

You must have the grace and love of God in order to succeed. The strength and spirituality of the people of God are manifest by the distinctness of the line of demarcation which separates them from the world. The people of the world are characterized by love for earthly things; they act selfishly, regardless of the principles which Christ has set forth in His life. Christians will manifest the self-sacrificing spirit of Christ in their work, in connection with every branch of the cause. They will do this heartily, not by halves. They will not study their own aggrandizement nor manifest respect of persons. They will not, cannot, live in luxury and self-indulgence while there are suffering ones around them. They cannot by their practice sanction any phase of oppression or injustice to the least child of humanity. There are to be like Christ, to relinquish all selfish delights, all unholy passions, all that love of applause which is the food of the world. They will be willing to be humble and unknown, and to sacrifice even life itself for Christ's sake. By a well-ordered life and godly conversation they will condemn the folly, the impenitence, the idolatry, the iniquitous practices of the world.

The converting power of God must work a transformation of character in many who claim to believe the present truth, or they cannot fulfill the purpose of God. They are hearers but not doers of the word. Pure, unworldly benevolence will be developed in all who make Christ their personal Savior. There needs to be far less of self and more of Jesus. The church of Christ is ordained of God that its members shall be representatives of Christ's character. He says, "You have given yourselves to Me, and I give you to the world. I am the light of the world; I present you to the world as My representatives." As Christ in the fullest sense represents the Father, so we are to represent Christ. Let none of those who name the name of Christ be cowards in His cause. For Christ's sake stand as if looking within the open portals of the city of God.

Ellen G. White
Battle Creek, Michigan
March 20, 1891

Part 2

Counsels Regarding the Work in the South

Chapter 1

Words of Precaution Regarding Sunday Labor

The Colored People, and the Way to Oppose Error. (Report of the Interview)

On the morning of November 20, 1895, a council meeting was called at the large tent on the Armadale campground to consider some questions arising from the discussions of our brethren regarding the religious liberty work. The positions recently taken by some of our brethren indicated that there was necessity for a more thorough understanding of the principles which must govern our work.

There were present brethren W. W. Prescott, A. G. Daniells, W. C. White, M. C. Israel, L. J. Rousseau, W. A. Colcord, M. G. Kellogg, W. D. Salisbury, James Smith, and sisters E. G. White and E. J. Burnham.

Several letters were read with reference to the questions at issue, then Sister White read a letter which she had written to Elder A. T. Jones, in May, 1894, which had been unavoidably withheld until very recently.

In this letter reference was made to the necessity of our speakers presenting the truth in such a simple manner that even the small children could comprehend the lessons which it was designed to teach. Remarking on this, Sister White said: "According to the light which has been given to me, when the heavenly intelligences see that men will no longer present the truth in simplicity as did Jesus, the very children will be moved upon by the spirit of God, and will go forth proclaiming the truth for this time."

The brethren were invited to discuss the points treated in the letters, but all were desirous of hearing further from Sister White, and she made the following remarks:

> "There is a terrible crisis just before us, through which all must pass, and especially will it come and be felt in Battle Creek. My mind has been much troubled over the positions which some of our brethren are liable to take in regard to the work to be done among the colored people in the Southern States. There is one point that I wish to lay before those who work in the Southern field. Among the colored people they will have to labor in different lines from those followed in the North. They cannot go to the South and present the real facts in reference to Sundaykeeping being the mark of the beast, and encourage the colored people to work on Sunday; for the same spirit that held the colored people in slavery is not dead, but alive today, and ready to spring into activity. The same spirit of oppression is still cherished in the minds of many of the white people of the South, and will reveal itself in cruel deeds, which are the manifestation of their religious zeal. Some will oppose in every possible way any action which has a tendency to uplift the colored race and teach them to be self-supporting."

> "When the whites show an inclination to help the colored people by educating them to help themselves, a certain class of the white people are terribly annoyed. They do not want the colored people to earn an independent living. They want them to work their plantations."

> "When the white people try to educate the colored people in the truth, jealousy is aroused, and ministers, both colored and white,

will bitterly oppose the truth. The colored ministers think that they know how to preach to their own race better than the white ministers can, and they feel that the whites are taking the work out of their hands. By falsehood they will create the most decided opposition, and those among the white people who are opposed to the truth will help them, and will make it exceedingly hard for the work of the message to advance."

"When the truth is proclaimed in the South, a marked difference will be shown by those who oppose the truth in their greater regard for Sunday, and great care must be exercised not to do anything to arouse their prejudice. Otherwise, we may just as well leave the field entirely, for the workers will have all the white people against them. Those who oppose the truth will not work openly, but through secret organizations, and they will seek to hinder the work in every possible way. Our laborers must move in a quiet way, striving to do everything possible to present the truth to the people, remembering that the love of Christ will melt down the opposition."

"From the light that I have received, I see that if we would get the truth before the Southern people, we must not encourage the colored people to work on Sunday. There must be a clear understanding regarding this, but it need not be published in our papers. You must teach these people as you would teach children. Not a word should be spoken to create prejudice, for if by any careless or impulsive speech to the colored people in regard to the whites any prejudice is created in their minds against the whites, or in the minds of the whites against them, the spirit of the enemy will work in the children of disobedience. Thus an opposition will be aroused which will hinder the work of the message, and will endanger the lives of the workers and of the believers."

THE SOUTHERN WORK

"We are not to make efforts to teach the Southern people to work on Sunday. That which some of our brethren have written upon this point is not based upon right principles. When the practices of the people do not come in conflict with the law of God, you may conform to them. If the workers fail to do this, they will not only hinder their own work, but they will place stumbling blocks in the way of those for whom they labor, and hinder them from accepting the truth. On Sunday there is the very best opportunity for those who are missionaries to hold Sunday schools, and come to the people in the simplest manner possible, telling them of the love of Jesus for sinners and educating them in the scriptures. There are many ways of reaching all classes, both white and black. We are to interest them in the life of Christ from his childhood up to manhood, and through his life of ministry to the cross. We cannot work in all localities in the same way. We must let the Holy Spirit guide, for men and women cannot convince others of the wrong traits of character. While laboring to introduce the truth, we must accommodate ourselves as much as possible to the field and the circumstances of those for whom we labor."

Question: Should not those in the Southern field work on Sunday?

"If they do this, there is danger that as soon as the opposing element can get the slightest opportunity, they will stir up one another to persecute those who do this and to pick off those whom they hate. At present Sundaykeeping is not the test. The time will come when men will not only forbid Sunday work, but they will try to force men to labor on the Sabbath. And men will be asked to renounce the Sabbath and to subscribe to Sunday observance or forfeit their freedom and their lives. But the time for this has not yet come, for the truth must be presented more fully before the people as a witness. What I have said about this should not be

understood as referring to the action of old Sabbathkeepers who understand the truth. They must move as the Lord shall direct them, but let them consider that they can do the best missionary work on Sunday...."

"It will not do for those who labor among the colored people to preach the truth as boldly and openly as they would be free to do in other places. Even Christ clothed his lessons in figures and parables to avoid the opposition of the Pharisees. When the colored people feel that they have the word of God in regard to the sabbath question, and the sanction of those who brought them the truth, some who are impulsive will take the opportunity to defy the Sunday laws, and by a presumptuous defiance of their oppressors they will bring to themselves much sorrow. Very faithfully the colored people must be instructed to be like Christ, to patiently suffer wrongs, that they may help their fellow men to see the light of truth."

"A terrible condition of things is certainly opening before us. According to the light which is given me in regard to the southern field, the work there must be done as wisely and carefully as possible, and it must be done in the manner in which Christ would work. The people will soon find out what you believe about Sunday and the Sabbath, for they will ask questions. Then you can tell them, but not in such a manner as to attract attention to your work. You need not cut short your work by yourself laboring on Sunday. It would be better to take that day to instruct others in regard to the love of Jesus and true conversion."

Question: Should the same principles govern our work and our attitude toward the Sunday question in foreign fields where the prejudices of the people are so strong?

"Yes; just the same. The light that I have is that God's servants should go quietly to work, preaching the grand, precious truths of the Bible—Christ and him crucified, his love and infinite sacrifice— showing that the reason why Christ died is because the law of God is immutable, unchangeable, eternal. The Spirit of the Lord will awaken the conscience and the understanding of those with whom you work, bringing the commandments of God to their remembrance. I can hardly describe to you the way in which this has been presented to me." The Lord says in Revelation 22:16: "I Jesus have sent mine angel to testify unto you these things in the churches." Have any of you seen this angel? The messengers from heaven are close beside those who stand before the people, holding forth the word of life. In preaching the truth, it is not always best to present those strong points of truth that will arouse prejudice, especially where such strong feelings exist as is felt in the southern states. The Sabbath must be taught in a decided manner, but be cautious how you deal with the idol, Sunday. A word to the wise is sufficient.

"I have given you the light which has been presented to me. If followed, it will change the course of many, and will make them wise, cautious teachers. Refraining from work on Sunday is not receiving the mark of the beast; and where this will advance the interests of the work, it should be done. We should not go out of our way to work on Sunday."

"After the Sabbath has been sacredly observed, in places where the opposition is so strong as to arouse persecution if work is done on Sunday, let our brethren make that day an occasion to do genuine missionary work. Let them visit the sick and the poor, ministering to their wants, and they will find favorable opportunities to open the scriptures to individuals and to families. Thus most profitable work can be done for the master. When those who hear and see the light on the Sabbath take their stand upon the truth to keep God's holy day, difficulties will arise, for efforts will be brought to bear

against them to compel men and women to transgress the law of God. Here they must stand firm, that they will not violate the law of God, and if the opposition and persecution are determinedly kept up, let them heed the words of Christ, 'when they persecute you in this city, flee ye into another: for verily I say unto you, ye shall not have gone over the cities of Israel, till the son of man be come."

"The time has not yet come for us to work as though there were no prejudice." Christ said, "be ye therefore wise as serpents, and harmless as doves." If you see that by doing certain things which you have A perfect right to do, you hinder the work of the truth, refrain from doing these things. Do nothing that will close the minds of others against the truth. There is a world to save, and we gain nothing by cutting loose from those we are trying to help. All things may be lawful, but all things are not expedient."

"We have no right to do anything that will obstruct the light which is shining from heaven; yet by a wrong course of action we may imperil the work, and close the door which God has opened for the entrance of the truth. The final issue on the Sabbath question has not yet come, and by imprudent actions we may bring on a crisis before the time. You may have all the truth, but you need not let it all flash at once upon minds, lest it become darkness to them. Even Christ said to his disciples, 'I have many things to say unto you, but ye can not bear them now.' We must not go into a place, open our satchels, show all we have, and tell everything that we know at once. We must work cautiously, presenting the truth by degrees, as the hearers can bear it, but keep close to the word."

(*Manuscript 22a*, 1895)
Published in The Southern Work, 128-136.

Ellen G. White

Chapter 2

Proper Methods of Work in the Southern Field

Note: Ellen G. White letter addressed to Elder A. O. Tait of Battle Creek, Michigan, recording secretary of the International Religious Liberty Association. The entire letter, except the sentence in parentheses just before the signature, was published by Elder O. A. Olsen, president of the General Conference, on November 22, 1896, as one of several items in Special Testimonies, Series A 6:47-56. It was subsequently reprinted by James Edson White in The Southern Work, 97-108.]

White Trustees
Armadale, Melbourne, Victoria, Australia,
November 20, 1895.

Dear Brother ——,

This morning I attended a meeting where a select few were called together to consider some questions that were presented to them by a letter soliciting consideration and advice on these subjects. Of some of these subjects I could speak, because at sundry times and in divers places many things have been presented to me in reference to some matters of labor that required great caution in speech as well as in the expression of thoughts with the pen. The advice given to our brethren in the Southern field has been diverse; it would bring in confusion.

As my brethren read the selections from letters, I knew what to say to them; for this matter has been presented to me again and again in regard to the Southern field. I have not felt at liberty to write out the matter until now. I will endeavor to make some brief statements at this time, hoping soon to have an opportunity to speak more clearly and at length.

The light that the Lord has given me at different times has been that the Southern field, where the greatest share of the population of the colored race is, cannot be worked after the same methods as other fields. They are excitable, and outward actions in bodily exercise more than inward piety, compose their religion. Should the colored people in the Southern States be educated, as they receive the truth, that they should work on Sunday, there would be excited a most unreasonable and unjust prejudice. Judges and jurors, lawyers and citizens, would, if they had a chance, bring decisions which would bind about them rites which would cause much suffering, not only to the ones whom they term guilty of breaking the laws of their State, but all the colored people everywhere would be placed in a position of surveillance, and under cruel treatment by the white people, that would be no less than slavery. They have been treated as chattels, regarded as not much above the dumb animals, to do just as their masters told them to do. This has degraded all their powers, and a different method of labor altogether must be pursued toward them than where the colored people have had greater advantages of schooling and have learned to read.

As the colored people have not been educated to read and have not been uplifted, their religion is more of bodily exercise than inward piety. There cannot be anything like the kind of labor pursued toward them that is bestowed upon the people whose religion is not outward workings. The Lord will look upon this poor, neglected, downtrodden race with great compassion. Everything of a character to set them in a position of opposition to authorities, as working on Sunday, would cause the colored people great suffering and cut off the possibility of the white laborers' going among them; for the workers who intended to do them good would be charged with raising insurrections.

I do not want anything of this character to appear, for I know the result. Tell them they need not provoke their neighbors by doing work on Sunday; that this will not prevent them from observing the Sabbath. The Sabbath should not be introduced until they know the first principles of the religion of Jesus Christ. The truth as it is in Jesus is to be made known little by little, line upon line, and precept upon precept.

Punishment for any offense would be visited unsparingly and unmercifully upon the colored people. Here is a neglected field, rank with corruption, needing to be taught everything; here is a field where medical missionary work can be one of the greatest blessings. In this line the truth may be introduced, but the very first principles of Christianity are to be taught in the A B C. Schools are to be established, having not only children, but fathers and mothers, learning to read.

Teaching the truth is involving great liabilities. It is essential, then, that families should settle in the South, and as missionary workers they can by precept and example be a living power. There cannot be much preaching. The least notice possible should be given to the point of what is doing and what is to be done; for it will create suspicion and jealousy in the minds of men, who, with their fathers and grandfathers, have been slaveholders. There has been so little done for the colored people that they are in moral degradation, and are looked upon as slaves to the white population still, although they have been emancipated at terrible cost.

We are to study the situation with great care, for the Lord is our enlightener. The Lord has given men capabilities to exercise, but there is too little deep thinking and too little earnest praying that the Lord would give wisdom at all times how to work difficult fields. We are under obligation to God, and if we love God, we are in duty bound not only on the general ground of obligation and obedience to obey the orders of our spiritual Leader, but to save as many souls as we can, to present them as sheaves to Jesus Christ, who gave Himself a living sacrifice to ransom them and make them free servants of Jesus Christ. There is not to be one word uttered which would stir up the slumbering enmity and hatred of the slaves against discipline and order, or to present before them the injustice that has been done them.

Nothing can be done at first in making the Sabbath question prominent, and if the colored people are in any way educated to work on Sunday, there will be unsparing, merciless oppression brought upon them. Already there has been too much printed in regard to the persecution of the Sabbathkeepers in the Southern States, and those who are bitter against the law of God, trampling it under their feet, are all the more in earnest to make human laws a power. Their religious prejudice and bigotry would lead them to do any act of violence, verily thinking they were doing God's service, for they are in great error. A blind zeal under false religious theories is the most violent and merciless. There are many who are stirred up by the representations in our papers to do just as their neighboring States are doing. All these things give them the appearance of defying the law. In Christ's day, when persecuted in one city, they fled to another. It may be the duty of those persecuted to locate themselves in another city or another country. "And ye shall be hated of all men for my name's sake: but he that endureth to the end shall be saved. But when they persecute you in this city, flee ye into another: for verily I say unto you, Ye shall not have gone over the cities of Israel, till the Son of man be come. The disciple is not above his master, nor the servant above his lord." (Matthew 10:22-24)

At present, persecution is not general, but let the Southern element have words come to them of a nature to arouse their excitable disposition, and the whole cause of truth would suffer and the great missionary field be closed. Let all be warned. Let the instruction be given to this much-oppressed people that the keeping of the Sabbath does not necessitate their working on Sunday; for if they should do this, they would have instigated against them all the powers of the white population who are transgressors of the law of God. Church members and priests and rulers will combine to organize secret societies to work in their land to whip, imprison, and destroy the lives of the colored race. History will be repeated. Let efforts be made in as silent a manner as possible, but this people need not be told that the observance of Sunday is the mark of the beast until this time shall come. If the Southern people get some of the ideas in their minds of the mark of the beast, they would misconstrue and give, honestly, the most false impression on these subjects and do strange things.

As many of the people cannot read for themselves, there are plenty of professed leaders who will read the Bible falsely, and make it testify to a lie. Many are working in this line now among those who are poor scholars, and have not a knowledge of the Scriptures. Our publications also will be misread. Things will be read out of the books that were never there, advocating the most objectionable things. An excitement could be easily worked up against Seventh-day Adventists. The most successful methods are to encourage families who have a missionary spirit to settle in the Southern States and work with the people without making any noise.

In such places as the Southern field there should be established sanitariums. There should be those who believe the truth—colored servants of God—under training to do work as medical missionaries under the supervision of white managers; for this combination will be much more successful. The medical missionary workers, cooperating with families who shall make their home in the South, need not think that God will condemn them if they do not work on Sunday; for the Lord understands that every effort must be made *not* to create prejudice, if the truth finds standing place in the South. The words of truth cannot go forth with great publicity, but schools should be started by families coming into the South and working in schools, not with a large number congregated in one school, but as far as possible in connection with those who have been working in the South. Dwell particularly upon the love of God, the righteousness of Christ, and the open treasure house of God, presenting the truth in clear lines upon personal piety. There will be the bad influence of the white people upon the blacks as there has been in the past. Evil angels will work with their own spirit upon evil men. Those cooperating with those who work in any place to uplift Jesus and to exalt the law of God, will find to all intents and purposes that they wrestle not against flesh and blood, but against principalities, against the rulers of the darkness of this world, and against spiritual wickedness in high places.

"Wherefore take unto you the whole armor of God, that ye may be able to withstand in the evil day, and having done all, to stand. Stand therefore, having your loins girt about with truth, and having on the breastplate of righteousness; and your feet shod with the preparation of the gospel of peace; above all, taking the shield of faith, wherewith ye shall be able to quench all the fiery darts of the wicked. And take the helmet of salvation, and the sword of the Spirit, which is the word of God."

Here is our sufficiency. Our defense is in the preparation of the gospel. The Lord will give wisdom to all who ask Him, but let those who are to work difficult and peculiar fields study Christ's methods. Let not their own peculiar traits of character be brought into the work; for Satan knows upon just what traits of character to work, that objectionable features may be revealed. These traits of character, received by inheritance or cultivated, are to be cut away from the soul, and the Spirit of Christ is to take possession of the organs of speech, of the mental power, of the physical and moral powers, else when in the midst of important interests Satan shall work with his masterly power to create a condition of things that will call into active exercise these special traits of character, and will bring defeat just when there should be a victory, and so the cause of God will sustain a loss.

"And unto the Jews I became as a Jew, that I might gain the Jews; to them that are under the law, as under the law, that I might gain them that are under the law; to them that are without law, as without law, (being not without law to God, but under the law to Christ) that I might gain them that are without law. To the weak became I as weak, that I might gain the weak: I am made all things to all men, that I might by all means save some. And this I do for the gospel's sake, that I might be partaker thereof with you." We know that the apostle did not sacrifice one jot of principle. He did not allow himself to be led away by the sophistry and maxims of men. He was not to coincide with the suppositions and assurances of men who were teaching for doctrine the commandments of men; because iniquity and transgression were in the ascendancy and advancing, he did not allow his love to wax cold. All zeal and earnestness are to be retained; but at the same time some features of our faith, if expressed, would, by the elements with which you have to deal, arouse prejudice at once.

Paul could be as zealous as any of the most zealous in his allegiance to the law of God, and show that he was perfectly familiar with the Old Testament Scriptures. He could dwell upon the types and shadows that typified Christ; he could exalt Christ, and tell all about Christ, and His special work in behalf of humanity, and what a field he had to explore. He could advance most precious light upon the prophecies, that they had not seen; and yet he would not offend them. Thus the foundation was laid nicely, that when the time came that their spirits softened, he could say in the language of John, Behold in Jesus Christ, who was made flesh, and dwelt among us, the Lamb of God, who taketh away the sins of the world.

To the Gentiles, he preached Christ as their only hope of salvation but did not at first have anything definite to say upon the law. But after their hearts were warmed with the presentation of Christ as the gift of God to our world, and what was comprehended in the work of the Redeemer in the costly sacrifice to manifest the love of God to man, in the most eloquent simplicity he showed that love for all mankind—Jew and Gentile—that they might be saved by surrendering their hearts to Him. Thus when, melted and subdued, they gave themselves to the Lord, he presented the law of God as the test of their obedience. This was the manner of working—adapting his methods to win souls. Had he been abrupt and unskillful in handling the Word, he would not have reached either Jew or Gentile.

He led the Gentiles along to view the stupendous truths of the love of God, who spared not His own Son, but delivered Him up for us; and how shall He not, with Him also freely give us all things? The question was asked why such an immense sacrifice was required, and then he went back to the types, and down through the Old Testament Scripture, revealing Christ in the law, and they were converted to Christ and to the law.

"But the wisdom that is from above is first pure, then peaceable, gentle, and easy to be intreated, full of mercy and good fruits, without partiality, and without hypocrisy. And the fruit of righteousness is sown in peace of them that make peace." All this may be, and yet not one principle of truth be sacrificed.

(I would not advise that this be published in our papers, but let the workers have it in leaflets, and let them keep their own counsels.) (*Letter 73*, 1895)

Ellen G. White

Chapter 3

Letter to A. O. Tait about the Southern Field

"Sunnyside," Cooranbong, N.S.W.,
March 2, 1897.

    The Southern field is a hard field, a very unsightly field, because it has been so long uncultivated. All who take hold of the work in the cause of God and suffering humanity will have to be one in their designs and plans. They will have plenty of trials and discouragements to meet, but they must not allow these to hinder or dishearten or handicap them in their work. In love for Christ, who died to save this poor, downtrodden people, in love for the souls of the perishing thousands, they are to labor for this worse than heathen country.

    Brethren, you have a work to do which you have left undone. A long-neglected field stands out in plain view before God to shame the people who have light and advanced truth but who have done so little to remove the stones and the rubbish that have been accumulating for so long a time. Those who have enjoyed every privilege and blessing have passed by on the other side. As a Christian people, God has called you to prepare the way of the Lord in this unpromising field. God sent a message to Nineveh by his servant Jonah, saying, "Arise, go to Nineveh, that great city, and cry against it; for their wickedness is come up before me." "And the word of the Lord came unto Jonah the second time, saying, Arise, go unto Nineveh, that great city, and preach unto it the preaching I bid thee. So Jonah arose, and went unto Nineveh, according to the word of the Lord. Now Nineveh was an exceeding great city of three days' journey. And Jonah began to enter into the city a day's journey, and he cried, and said, Yet forty days, and Nineveh shall be overthrown."

When the people of Nineveh humbled themselves before God and cried to Him for mercy, He heard their cry. "God saw their works, that they turned from their evil way; and God repented of the evil, that he said he would do unto them; and he did it not." But Jonah revealed that he did not value the souls in that wretched city. He valued his reputation, lest they should say that he was a false prophet. He said, "O Lord, was not this my saying, when I was yet in my country? Therefore I fled before unto Tarshish: for I knew that thou art a gracious God, and merciful, slow to anger, and of great kindness, and repentest thee of the evil." Now when he sees the Lord exercise His compassionate attributes, and spare the city that had corrupted its ways before Him, Jonah does not cooperate with God in His merciful design. He has not the people's interests in view. It does not grieve him that so large a number must perish, who have not been educated to do right. Listen to his complaint:

> "Therefore, now, O Lord, take, I beseech thee, my life from me; for it is better for me to die than to live. Then said the Lord, Doest thou well to be angry? So Jonah went out of the city, and sat on the east side of the city, and there made him a booth, and sat under it in the shadow, till he might see what would become of the city. And the Lord prepared a gourd, and made it come up over Jonah, that it might be a shadow over his head, to deliver him from his grief. So Jonah was exceeding glad of the gourd."

Then the Lord gave Jonah an object lesson. He prepared a worm when the morning sun rose next day, and it smote the gourd that it withered. "And it came to pass, when the sun did rise, that God prepared a vehement east wind; and the sun beat upon the head of Jonah, that he fainted, and wished in himself to die, and said, It is better for me to die than to live. And God said to Jonah, Doest thou well to be angry for the gourd? And he said, I do well to be angry, even unto death. Then said the Lord, Thou hast had pity on the gourd, for the which thou hast not labored, neither madest it grow; which came up in a night, and perished in a night; and should I not spare Nineveh, that great city, wherein are more than sixscore thousand persons that cannot discern between their right hand and their left hand; and also much cattle?"

In the history of Nineveh there is a lesson which you should study carefully. This lesson is to be learned for yourselves, and in regard to your relation to the Southern States. You must know your duty to your fellow beings who are ignorant and defiled and who need your help. The Southern field is a hard field, but is this any excuse for your doing scarcely anything for it? Read the eighth and ninth chapters of Second Corinthians. Study and heed these lessons, for you need such examples kept ever before you. The Lord is not pleased with your treatment of the Southern field.... What deep humiliation should be felt by those whom God has so greatly favored with His blessing of light, whom He has made the repositories of truth, the most sacred truth ever given to our world, but who have neglected their God-given work. What far-seeing judgment they would now have if at the heart of the work men had been careful to seek their counsel from God as to who should connect with His great work to prepare a people to stand in these last days against principalities, against powers, against the rulers of the darkness of this world, against spiritual wickedness in high places....

The deepest humility should be felt by those who have the privileges of enlightenment and education in missionary lines. The Lord God of heaven, by whom all actions are weighed in the golden balances of the sanctuary, looks upon the thousands of colored people, our neighbors, who in their destitution are spreading their cases before the Giver of all mercies and blessings. These people are perishing in their sins. As a people they are ignorant, many knowing nothing of purity and godliness and elevation. But among them are men and women of quick perceptions, excellent talents, and these will be revealed when once the Spirit of God shall turn their attention to the Word. But they need ministry not in the Word alone. Those who would do God service in this field must go among the people.

There are those who, while they profess godliness, are not pure. They have corrupted their ways before God. And when these people meet those who have no disguise for their corruption, they have so little sense of what constitutes a high and holy character that they are in danger of revealing that they are of a class as degraded as their fellow beings of the Southern States. The people of the South do not need those to go among them who have not the love of the truth in their hearts, and who will easily yield to temptation, who, with all the light they have, will descend to the low level of the moral corruption of those they are professedly trying to save. This will be the danger of those whose minds are not pure, therefore be sure that men of steadfast principle be sent to work for God in this field.

In His providence God is saying as He has been saying for years past: Here is a field for you to work. Those who are wise in agricultural lines, in tilling the soil, those who can construct simple, plain buildings, may help. They can do good work and at the same time show in their characters the high morality which it is the privilege of this people to attain to. Teach them the truth in simple object lessons.

Make everything upon which they lay their hands a lesson in character building. The South is calling to God for temporal and spiritual food, but it has been so long neglected that hearts have become hard as stone. God's people need now to arouse and redeem their sinful neglect and indifference of the past. These obligations now rest heavily upon the churches, and God will graciously pour out His Spirit upon those who will take up their God-given work. (*Manuscript 164*, 1897)

Ellen G. White

Part 3

Special Counsels and
Cautions in 1899

… Chapter 1

Colonization Not Advisable

"Sunnyside," Cooranbong,
June 5, 1899.

Dear Brother_____,
    I remember you distinctly, and I have rejoiced to see you growing in grace and working in the Lord's vineyard. I would say, my brother, you would best stand at your post of duty, laboring in the ministry of the Word.
    As you say, there is no more fruitful field than the South. It is the prejudice of the white against the black race that makes this field hard, very hard. The whites who have oppressed the colored people still have the same spirit. They did not lose it, although they were conquered in war. They are determined to make it appear that the blacks were better off in slavery than since they were set free. Any provocation from the blacks is met with the greatest cruelty. The field is one that needs to be worked with the greatest discretion. Any mingling of the white people with the colored people, as sleeping in their houses, or showing them friendship as would be shown by the whites to those of their own color, is exasperating to the white people of the South. Yet these same persons employ colored women to nurse their children, and further, not a few white men have had children by colored women. Thus the colored people have received an education from the whites in immorality, and many of them stand ready to treat the whites as the whites have treated

them. The relation of the two races has been a matter hard to deal with, and I fear that it will ever remain a most perplexing problem.

You speak of a way of helping the colored race in a way which does not excite the prejudice of the white Southern-born citizens; that is, the industrial school. As you have presented, the greatest caution needs to be exercised in regard to politics. Some persons are of such a temperament that they would make trouble by want of proper consideration. Words dropped unadvisedly would be like a spark, kindling a flame of intense jealousy and dangerous opposition. Whoever works in the South needs to be sanctified in body, soul, and spirit. Then there will be wise words, not words spoken at random or without duly weighing every expression.

It is from the whites that the greatest opposition may be expected. This is the quarter that we shall need to watch. The white people are prejudiced against the doctrines taught by the Seventh-day Adventists, and a religious opposition is the greatest difficulty. The white people will stir up the blacks by telling them all kinds of stories; and the blacks, who can lie even when it is for their interest to speak the truth, will stir up the whites with falsehoods, and the whites who want an occasion will seize upon any pretext for taking revenge, even upon those of their own color who are presenting the truth. This is the danger. As far as possible, everything that will stir up the race prejudice of the white people should be avoided. There is danger of closing the door so that our white laborers will not be able to work in some places in the South.

All that you have written in regard to the great necessity of the colored people is correct. I have seen that those who know the truth for this time have a special work to take up for this people. Christ came to our world, clothing His divinity with humanity, that He might work with humanity, fallen, degraded, corrupted. He came of poor parentage, and lived the life of a poor man. He was accustomed to privation. As a member of the family He acted His part in laboring with His hands for the support of His mother and His brothers and sisters. Thus He, the Majesty of heaven, was not to appear as honoring the greatest men because of their wealth. He has forever removed from poverty the disgrace which is attached to it because it is destitute of worldly advantages. He says, "The foxes have holes, and the birds of the air have nests; but the Son of man hath not where to lay his head."

[Two] thousand years ago a voice of strange and mysterious import was heard in heaven from the throne of God: "Sacrifice and offering thou didst not desire; mine ears hast thou opened: burnt offering and sin offering hast thou not required. Then said I, Lo, I come: in the volume of the book it is written of me, I delight to do thy will, O my God: yea, thy law is within my heart." Christ in counsel with His Father laid out the plan for His life on earth. It was not a chance, but a design that the world's Redeemer should lay off His crown, lay aside His kingly robe, and come to our world as a man. He clothed His divinity with the garb of humanity, that He might stand at the head of the human family, His humanity mingled with the humanity of the race fallen because of Adam's disobedience. The poverty and humiliation of the Son of the infinite God teach lessons that few care to learn. There is a link that connects Christ with the poor in a special sense. He, the life, the light of the world, makes poverty His own teacher, in order that He may be educated by the same stern, practical teacher as are the poor. Since the Lord Jesus accepted a life of poverty, no one can justly look with contempt upon the poor. The Savior of the world was the King of glory, and He stripped Himself of His glorious outward adorning, accepting poverty, that He might understand how the poor are treated in this world. He was afflicted in all the afflictions of the human family, and He pronounces His blessing, not upon the rich, but upon the poor of this world.

You speak of the Oakwood Industrial School for colored students as not having sufficient buildings to accommodate the students, twelve in number occupying one room. My brother, is it not the duty of someone laboring in this line to labor for the creation of a fund to supply this need? Let appeals be made to our people. Let each give a little, even among the poor. Without delay, encourage the brethren to erect

THE SOUTHERN WORK

a humble building large enough to accommodate the students. Ask the people to heed the words of Christ, "Whosoever will come after me, let him deny himself, and take up his cross, and follow me." The example of Christ is for our imitation.

Those who undertake work in the South must not enter into any plan for colonizing, for this will place them in perilous circumstances. Some families should be found who for Christ's sake will volunteer to enter the Southern field. At Huntsville there is a building, and something has been done there. Let the proper ones try to make that place different by bringing into it new, live elements. This plant must not become useless. Elements must be brought in which will make the institution self-sustaining. Then if it is necessary, cheap additions can be made.

I would not encourage your plan. It means much, very much more than you think, to obtain and improve hundreds of acres of land. Your aftersight in this matter would be very different from your foresight. This work for the Southern people will require the tact of the most ingenious Christian. In the past you have seen families settled in localities where they could work successfully for the spread of the truth, and you have thought that this same plan could be adopted for the work in the South. But your expectation will not be realized.

The expenses of such company in food and clothing must be considered. The results would not be such as you suppose. This plan will bring disappointment. Let each family who shall commit itself to the work, go as the Lord's missionaries, to work their own way. Workers are not to pledge themselves to five years' labor, for many will not bear the test. Some would find fault and complain, and thus sow the seed of evil surmising. These persons might work interestedly for a time, and then become dissatisfied and want a change. The Lord looks upon every heart. There are some souls you cannot trust. They are unreliable. In the company you would form you would find tares among the wheat. It would be better to begin work in Huntsville and make the work there a success.

I would say to you, my brother, that in the future nothing can be relied on in the Southern States. You cannot make settlements with the purpose of carrying on a large business, cultivating lands, and teaching the colored people how to work. At the least provocation the poison of prejudice is ready to show its true character, and provocations will be found. It is very hard to make the work run smoothly. Outbreaks will come at any moment, and all unexpectedly, and there will be destruction of property and even of life itself. Hot-headed people, professing the faith, but without judgment, will think they can do as they please, but they will find themselves in a tight place. I speak that which I know. Everyone takes his life in his hands by following such a course. There are some localities less perilous than others, but never can there be large settlements built up in the South. Every act is to be oiled with the grace of God, every word spoken, carefully studied. Parties are already formed, and they are waiting, burning with a desire to serve their master, the devil, and do abominable work. Professed Christians are more determined in these things than out-and-out sinners. (*Letter 90*, 1899)

Ellen G. White

Chapter 2

The Field Becoming Difficult

"Sunnyside," Cooranbong,
July 2, 1899.

Dear Brother_____,

In the South there are some places where work can be done. But the neglect of our people to respond to the light God has given has closed some openings which it will now be very difficult for them to enter. I inquire, What do our people mean by this neglect to work the Southern field? True, it is not a desirable field; and unless the Lord shall inspire with His love the hearts of His people, they will not succeed. They are not to begin by publishing the great and wonderful things they are going to do. Cannot they see that if they do this, the gate will be closed against them? That which might have been done years ago in the South cannot now be done.

When the children of Israel were encamped on the other side of the Jordan, "the Lord spake unto Moses, saying, Send thou men, that they may search the land of Canaan, which I give unto the children of Israel." Read this history, contained in the thirteenth and fourteenth chapters of Numbers. When the evil report brought back by the spies was received, God was displeased, and declared His determination concerning the people. For forty years they were to wander in the wilderness. After He had said this, the people decided to go up. But the favorable time had passed. The news of their coming had been circulated, and their enemies were prepared to resist them. And Moses said, "Go not up, for the Lord is not among you; that ye be not smitten before your enemies." But they presumptuously went to the hilltop to be defeated by their enemies.

Thus it is now with some places in the South. The doors are closed. Yet there are other places where prejudice has not been excited, and where work may be done. I write this to our people that they may see that it is not knowledge that they need, but new hearts, cleansed from all selfishness and covetousness. Those who have had every facility and convenience have shown their neglect for fields which have had so little. In some parts of the Lord's vineyard nothing has been done. Money has been raised and appropriated, although not for personal advantage, yet in distinct disobedience to the Lord's requirements. Those parts of His great vineyard where the least has been done were to be worked; but methods were used to divert the means for this purpose into other channels. Through misrepresentation and misinterpretation the Southern field has been robbed. That field has not received from the Lord's treasury its meat in due season.

The men whose influence cut off every advantage in the publication of books the profits of which were to be used in the Southern field, might better examine themselves and see what they have done in working out false theories and principles, which have brought upon the workers in our institutions the frown of God. O I beg of every soul who has connived in these matters, to repent and confess and be converted, sending their sins beforehand to judgment.

My brother, I will send you that which I have in regard to the Southern field. The plans and efforts that could have been made years ago will not now succeed in some places. It is best to move when the Lord sends word to move, and not study human minds, human methods, human plans, human convenience. The Lord is wearied with the unbelief, selfishness, and covetousness of His people. This has stood in the way of the advancement of His work.

Eighty thousand dollars, I understand, were invested in the sanitarium in Boulder, pressing upon the heart of the work a heavier load of debt than was already there. Did the Lord devise that work? No; that amount of money was needed in India, in Australia, in the Southern field, in foreign fields, that the Lord's ministers might carry the message of truth to places nigh which have never been worked, and to places afar off.

The Lord is displeased with His people, because they have worked at cross-purposes with Him. Money has been invested in various conveniences and facilities which the Lord never directed. There is earnest work to be done, but the money is consumed, so that the will of God is not done. My heart is sick and sore and distressed beyond measure. May the Lord awaken His people, who are not yet half awake.

I have thought of Paul, the great minister who was sent to preach Christ and Him crucified to the Gentiles. On one occasion he was in a strait betwixt two. He was so weighed down with responsibilities that he knew not whether he would rather die or live, whether he would choose for the good of others to abide in the flesh or give up the conflict. "Brethren," he writes, "I count not myself to have apprehended: but this one thing I do, forgetting those things which are behind, and reaching forth unto those things which are before, I press toward the mark for the prize of the high calling of God in Christ Jesus."

My brother, walk humbly with God. I wish that the work could have been done in the Southern field which God designed should be done; but men have proved untrustworthy stewards. May the Lord give His people hearts of flesh, and not hearts of steel, is my prayer. (*Letter 100*, 1899)

Ellen G. White

Chapter 3

Further Counsel Regarding a Colony in the South

The following is taken from a private letter to Mr. and Mrs. J. E. White, written June 21, 1899.

Brother ⸺ has sent me a letter in regard to his plans for the South, but I cannot encourage such plans. He will calculate to have all things move smoothly. A community to settle in the South in accordance with the plans he has thought would prove a success, would prove a failure. What is the prospect for feeding and clothing this community? Where is the money to be pledged for building homes for families? The outlay would be greater than the income. There would be a gathering of good and bad, there would be the need of men of clear conception, baptized with the Holy Spirit of God, to run such an enterprise. I might present many things that make it objectionable. There cannot be any colonizing without Satan stirring up the Southern element to look with suspicion on the Northern people, and the least provocation would awaken the Southern whites to produce a state of things they do not now imagine.

There must be laborers in the South who possess caution. They must be wise as serpents and harmless as doves. All who engage in this work should be men who have their pens and tongues dipped in the holy oil of Zechariah 4:11-14. An unadvised word will stir the most violent passions of the human heart and set in operation a state of things that will close the way for the truth to find access to the fields now in such great need of workers.

It is not ministers who can preach that are needed so much as men and women who understand how to teach the truth to poor, ignorant, needy, and oppressed people. And as to making it appear that there is not need of caution, it is because those who say such things do not know what they are talking about. It needs men and women who will not be *sent* to the Southern field by our people, but who will feel the burden to go into this neglected portion of the vineyard of the Lord. Men, while their hearts burn with indignation as they see the attitude of the white people toward the black, will learn of the Master, Jesus Christ, that silence in expression regarding these things is eloquence. They all need the intelligence that will lead them to learn of Jesus Christ and the simplicity of how to work.

The cultivation of the soil is an excellent arrangement, but it is not by Northern people grouping together in a community that will accomplish the work they imagine will be a success. Hot-tempered men better remain in the North. Men and women who possess the true Christlike spirit of ministry may do excellent work among the Southern colored people. Make no masterly efforts to break down the prejudices of the Southern people, but just live and talk the love of Jesus Christ. There cannot be any greater harm done to the Southern colored people than to dilate on the harm and wrong done them by the white Southerners.

There is need of level-headed men and women who love the Lord Jesus, and who will love the colored people for Christ's sake, who have the deepest pity for them. But the methods of Sister S_____ are not the methods that will be wise to practice. They cannot be petted and treated just as if they were on a level with the whites without ruining them for all missionary work in the Southern field. There is a difference among the blacks as there is among the whites. Some possess keen and superior talents, that if the possessor is not made too much of, and is treated from a Bible standpoint, as humble men to do a Christlike missionary work, not exalting them, but teaching them religious love, and Christlike love for the souls of their own colored race, and keep before them that they are not called into the field to labor for the whites, but to learn to labor in the love of God to restore the moral image of God in those of their own race, then a good work can be done.

There is a work to be done in opening schools to teach the colored people alone, unmixed with whites, and there will be a successful work done in this way. The Lord will work through the whites to reach the black race—many of them through white teachers, but it needs the man and his wife to stand together in the work. More than one family of white teachers should locate in a place. Two or three families should locate near each other, not huddle together, but at a little distance apart, where they can consult together and unite in worship of God together, and work to strengthen each other's hands to raise up colored laborers to work in the South.

There is a mistake often made by those who labor in the Southern fields expecting that their brethren in the Northern fields of labor can advise them what to do. Those who have had no experience in the Southern field are not prepared to give reliable advice. Those who are engaged in this work must understand that when emergencies arise they must not depend upon men who have had no experience to advise them. They will often obtain advice that if followed would be ruinous to the work. Therefore it is not good policy for one family alone to settle in a locality. Men and women who have not children are best qualified for the Southern field, and if the Southern field is too taxing or debilitating, one family from the two or three who have settled in a locality can be spared. But let none feel that it is their bounden duty to remain in the Southern field after their health has testified that they cannot do this safely. Some persons can endure the climate and do well. But let our brethren in the more favorable climate consider all these things and provide every facility possible to make the conditions of workers in these unfavorable locations as pleasant as possible.

In places where money has been expended on buildings, and a start has been made, it is the duty of men in responsible positions to give attention to that locality, so that the workers shall be sustained in accomplishing the work designed when the plant was made. There is to be a work done in the South, and it needs men and women who will not need to be preachers so much as teachers—humble men who are not afraid to work as farmers to educate the Southerners how to till the soil, for whites and blacks need to be educated in this line. But when perplexities arise in the South, spread out your wants to the Master of the vineyard. And those who know nothing of the Southern field, let them be sparing and cautious what advice they give. But sympathy, kind words, and encouragement are always in place. (*Letter 102a*, 1899)

Ellen G. White

Chapter 4

A Neglected Work

April 27, 1899.

I cannot sleep past eleven o'clock. Several times I have had a pointed testimony in regard to the Southern field. After speaking on the subject of royalties in connection with book publication, she continues.

I awoke, but my soul was burdened. I felt that peculiar trials were to come upon the people of God. Then was presented before me the situation of the Southern field. The work which should have been done in that field has not been done. The means sent in by the people to the General Conference for the advancement of the work there was devoted to other purposes. This is where the work of restitution must be done. The Lord is displeased with the men in responsible positions who have not discerned the great need of this field. The work there needs means. God has given warnings, but they have not been heeded. Church members in America who have pleasant homes and surroundings should remember the Southern field. It is in need of special attention and support. I addressed the president of the General Conference, Why do you neglect this work? God has made it your duty to deal with this poor, oppressed race as their circumstances demand. Let the work go forward. Encourage the people who are favorably situated to help in this field. The Lord does not call families to work in the South who have young children who would thus be exposed to evil associations, but He calls those who can work to advantage in the different localities.

There are men who will tell you that the work in the South has been misrepresented, that it is not so arduous as it is made to appear. Let no one suppose that the Southern field is an easy place to work; for it is the most difficult portion of the Lord's vineyard, and soon it will be even more difficult. The greatest wisdom must be exercised. All connected with the work, and especially those who have to do with the publications sent to this field, must be as wise as serpents and as harmless as doves. Be careful what your pens shall trace for publication. There are many things which it will do only harm to make public.

If the greatest caution is not exercised, bitterness and hatred will be aroused in the white people in the South who are yearning for power to oppress the colored race as they have in the past. Those who are in the habit of speaking without consideration might far better remain in their homes than attempt work in this field. Those who think that the precautions given are unnecessary should heed the warnings the Lord has sent. If you would have a part in the work in the South, my brethren, you must hide self in Christ, walking humbly and circumspectly before God.

Common association with the blacks is not a wise course to pursue. To lodge with them in their homes may stir up feelings in the minds of the whites which will imperil the lives of the workers. Goods have been sent to this field which have helped to relieve the necessities of suffering humanity. But this work does not please the white people. In some localities they do not want help to be given to this downtrodden race. They desire that they shall ever feel their dependence.

I tell you of a truth that this field with its neglect will come up in judgment to condemn those who have been admonished, but who have refused to lend the aid. The Lord demands restitution from the churches in America. You are to relieve the necessities of this field. In the day of final accounts men will not be pleased to meet the record of their deeds with reference to the books that have been prepared to help in carrying on the work in the South, by which means was diverted from the most needy portion of the Lord's vineyard. This matter has been before you a long time, and what have you done to relieve the situation? Why have you kept so quiet? O that you would do this work of restoration speedily. The Lord calls upon you to restore to his people the advantages of which they have so long been deprived. The evil work done will one day be seen, not in the light in which responsible men now see it, who like the priest and Levite have passed by on the other side, but as God views it.

God's people have no excuse to offer as to why the years which have passed into eternity do not show better results. The way in which some of the teachers have managed the work in the South has not been right, and yet many have looked with great enthusiasm on the work of those who through incorrect methods have given a wrong mold to the work. Should these methods be encouraged? No; for the material worked upon is not being in the least qualified to help the Southern people.

The breaking down of distinctions between the white and the colored races unfits the blacks to work for their own class, and exerts a wrong influence upon the whites.

Again I place this matter before you. Will you act upon the light given? (*Manuscript 90*, 1899)

Ellen G. White

Chapter 5

Principles Regarding Restitution

(From a letter to Elder J. N. Loughborough, dated February 19, 1899.)

As regards the principle that should guide our people in such matters, I have been instructed that wherever by self-sacrifice and urgent labor the work necessary for the establishment and advancement of the cause has been done and facilities provided, and the Lord has prospered, those in that place should give of their means to help God's servants who have been sent to new fields to go over the same experience, beginning at the A B C of the work. Those living where the work has been established on a good foundation should feel themselves bound to help those in need, by transferring even at great self-sacrifice and self-denial a portion or all of the means which in former years was invested by those living at a distance in behalf of the work in their locality. Thus the Lord designs that the work shall increase. The talents given to his servants are to be doubled by being put out to use in gifts and offerings and the bestowal of influence.

This is the law of restitution on right lines. One portion of the Lord's vineyard is worked and brings in fruit. Then another portion is taken up, and it is the Lord's plan that the new, unworked part shall receive help from the part that has been worked. Thus the work in every part becomes a success. The help thus rendered should be given with cheerfulness. When the principles of the law of God are thus practiced, the work moves forward with solidity and double strength. Then the messengers are enabled with great power to proclaim the third angel's message and the soon appearing with power and great glory of our Lord and Savior Jesus Christ. (*Letter 35*, 1899)

Ellen G. White

ABOUT ELLEN G. WHITE

Ellen Gould Harmon White, a woman of remarkable spiritual gifts, was also one of the most prolific writers of all time. Though she lived the bulk of her life during the 19th century (1827-1915), her writings continue to make a revolutionary impact on millions of people today.

During her lifetime, Mrs. White wrote 40 books and more than 5,000 magazine articles. Since her death, a number of additional books have been compiled from her manuscripts. Today, Mrs. White is the most translated American author of all time and the most translated non-fiction female writer in the history of literature.

The writings of Mrs. White cover a broad range of topics, including Bible stories and studies, education, family relationships, health, prophecy, publishing, and much more. Steps to Christ, Mrs. White's life-changing masterpiece on successful Christian living, has been published in more than 140 languages.

Seventh-day Adventists believe that Mrs. White's books are of special value and significance. In the pages of the "little red books" (as they are sometimes called), Adventists see more than a gifted writer. They see a woman called by God. As a special messenger for this time, Mrs. White's job was to draw the world's attention to the Bible and help people prepare for the Second Coming of Jesus.

Between the ages of 17 and 87 years old, God gave Mrs. White approximately 2,000 dreams and visions. Some of the visions lasted for less than a minute; others spanned several hours. The counsel and knowledge received in these visions formed the basis for many of Mrs. White's writings. Her eloquent prose is recognized for its exceptional quality even by casual readers. Although Seventh-day Adventists believe the writings of Ellen White to be inspired, they are not seen as a replacement for the Bible.

Born in 1827 to Methodist parents in Gorham, Maine, Ellen White suffered a near-fatal accident at age 9 which disfigured her face for life. The accident, which resulted from a rock thrown by a classmate, was so severe that Ellen became sickly and was unable to continue her education. As a young person, Ellen was deeply disappointed in the direction her life had taken due to the injury. She found hope and a new lease on life, however, when she heard sermons by a Baptist preacher named William Miller proclaiming the soon coming of Jesus. Miller's preaching, which was part of the revival known as the "Great Awakening" that swept the world at that time, resulted in many (including Ellen White) believing that Jesus would come in 1843, and (when that didn't happen) in October of 1844.

The sermons of Miller, who was known for his powerful appeals to sinners to come to Christ, touched Ellen deeply. Preachers of that day were more likely to dwell on the agonies of an eternally burning hell in their sermons than they were to talk about the love and mercy of God. The famous sermon, "Sinners in the Hands of an Angry God" by Jonathan Edwards was a prime example of what many ministers served up every week. To the young Ellen, the love and mercy of God seemed like an unattainable dream.

Miller's preaching, together with the kind words of a godly Methodist minister and Ellen's mother, encouraged the young searcher and helped her to understand the love of God more fully. A dream Ellen had at about that time added to her feeling of hope and belief that Jesus loved her and would be merciful to her.

The summer after first hearing Miller's preaching, Ellen gave her heart fully to Jesus. As she experienced the sweet assurance that her sins were forgiven, joy filled her heart. Shortly after, she was baptized (by immersion) into the Methodist church. Once converted, Ellen took every opportunity she could to share the love of Jesus—and joy of salvation—with others. Working earnestly for the salvation of her circle of friends, Ellen sometimes stayed up and prayed for them all night long. In the end, and with Ellen's encouragement, all but one of her young friends surrendered their hearts to Jesus. In the Methodist "class meetings," which Ellen attended, she and her brother Robert loved to speak simply of the joy they felt in the hope of the soon return of Jesus. Their testimonies were not well received, however. In time, both Ellen and Robert found their names removed from the rolls of the Methodist Church.

When Jesus didn't come at the time predicted by the Millerites, Ellen, together with many other Advent believers, was deeply disappointed. The "Great Disappointment," as the experience came to be called, caused many to abandon their belief in the Second Coming. For Ellen and others, however, the disappointment was a turning point. As they dug more deeply into the Scriptures, they not only saw the error of time-setting, but came to love Jesus more.

It was during this time of soul-searching, in December of 1844, that Ellen had her first vision at the tender age of 17. Though shy about sharing at first, Ellen became convinced of the need to tell others about her visions. Ellen's testimony became a great encouragement to other believers since it bolstered their faith in the imminent return of Jesus. Although some of Ellen's visions were of heaven, she was also sometimes called to rebuke fanatics, a task which she found to be particularly hard.

In 1846, Ellen married a young evangelist named James White. James and Ellen also began to keep the Bible Sabbath at about this time. Ellen's first book, A Sketch of the Christian Experience and Views of Ellen G. White, was published in 1851.

As the ministry of the White's expanded, so did their family. In time, the couple had four children, all boys. Because of their many traveling commitments, the Whites had to be gone from their children quite a bit during those early years. This was a great sorrow, especially to Ellen. The grief of the young couple was compounded when they lost the youngest and oldest of their children (Hubert as an infant in 1860 and Henry at the age of 16 in 1863).

In 1855, just when James' health—and finances—were at a low point, the couple moved to Battle Creek, Michigan. It was there in Battle Creek that things began to turn around.

One of Ellen's most famous books, The Great Controversy Between Christ and Satan, was published in 1888. Another classic which tells the story of the life of Christ (The Desire of Ages) was first published in 1898.

In addition to publishing books, the Whites were involved in starting and publishing a magazine known as The Advent Review and Sabbath Herald. James was the founding editor of that publication, which is still in circulation (as the Adventist Review) today.

Throughout her long ministry, Ellen White continued to have many visions. In some of these visions, Mrs. White was shown future events before they occurred. For example, she saw the devastating 1906 San Francisco earthquake in vision two days before it actually took place. Mrs. White also had a vision of the American Civil War, and how terrible it would be, ahead of the conflict. At that time, many people expected little more than a skirmish. Sadly, the deadliness of the war, with certain details, were things that Mrs. White predicted with incredible accuracy.

In addition to penning many books and magazine articles, Mrs. White helped to found the Seventh-day Adventist Church. Her writings have been a blessing to thousands, perhaps millions. Many Bible students have found this remarkable woman to meet all the Biblical tests of a prophet as outlined in the Holy Scriptures.

Mrs. White continued to write, admonish, and minister until she fell and broke her hip in California at the age of 86. She died five months later on July 16, 1915. Three funerals were held in her honor, after which she was buried in Battle Creek, Michigan.

www.ingramcontent.com/pod-product-compliance
Lightning Source LLC
Chambersburg PA
CBHW070112080526
44586CB00013B/1272